COUNSELLING STUDENTS

BASIC TEXTS IN COUNSELLING AND PSYCHOTHERAPY

Series Editor: Stephen Frosh

This series introduces readers to the theory and practice of counselling and psychotherapy across a wide range of topic areas. The books will appeal to anyone wishing to use counselling and psychotherapeutic skills and will be particularly relevant to workers in health, education, social work and related settings. The books in this series are unusual in being rooted in psychodynamic and systemic ideas, yet being written at an accessible, readable and introductory level. Each text offers theoretical background and guidance for practice, with creative use of clinical examples.

Published

Jenny Altschuler
WORKING WITH CHRONIC ILLNESS

Bill Barnes, Sheila Ernst and Keith Hyde
AN INTRODUCTION TO GROUPWORK

Emilia Dowling and Gill Gorell Barnes
WORKING WITH CHILDREN AND PARENTS THROUGH
SEPARATION AND DIVORCE

Gill Gorell Barnes
FAMILY THERAPY IN CHANGING TIMES

Ravi Rana
COUNSELLING STUDENTS

Paul Terry
COUNSELLING THE ELDERLY AND THEIR CARERS

Jan Wiener and Mannie Sher
COUNSELLING AND PSYCHOTHERAPY IN PRIMARY HEALTH CARE

Forthcoming

Marilyn Lawrence and Mira Dana
COUNSELLING AND PSYCHOTHERAPY IN THE EATING DISORDERS

Adam Jukes
WORKING WITH MEN

Anne McFadyen
WORKING WITH CHILDREN WITH LEARNING DISABILITIES

Basic Texts in Counselling and Psychotherapy
Series Standing Order ISBN 0–333–69330–2
(outside North America only)

You can receive future titles in this series as they are published by placing a standing order. Please contact your bookseller or, in the case of difficulty, write to us at the address below with your name and address, the title of the series and the ISBN quoted above.

Customer Services Department, Macmillan Distribution Ltd.
Houndmills, Basingstoke, Hampshire RG21 6XS, England

COUNSELLING STUDENTS

A Psychodynamic Perspective

RAVI RANA

Foreword by Ellen Noonan

First published 2000 by
MACMILLAN PRESS LTD
Houndmills, Basingstoke, Hampshire RG21 6XS
and London
Companies and representatives
throughout the word

ISBN 0–333–79051–0

A catalogue record for this book is available
from the British Library.

This book is printed on paper suitable for recycling and
made from fully managed and sustained forest sources.

10   9   8   7   6   5   4   3   2   1
09 08 07 06 05 04 03 02 01 00

Printed in Malaysia

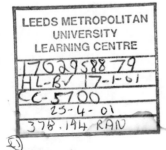

For Kawal and Sofia

CONTENTS

FOREWORD

Every summer now we read reports about record-breaking A-level results and the satisfying increase in the number of students going on to higher education. This is presented as an achievement for both our educational system and the individual students in the current results-oriented culture of evaluation, comparison, and quality assurance. Regardless of the debate about whether or not exams are getting easier, the mood is celebratory and congratulatory: all those fortunate young people can avail themselves of the opportunity of a university education. They are set for the 'time of their lives', can lay the foundation for brilliant careers in the fields of their choice, and will meet the people who become lifelong friends and partners. Behind the scenes, true, there are those whose results were disappointing, requiring them to scrabble through 'clearing' for a place that is at least acceptable, thus launching their university career with a mixture of rejection and relief. Waiting for them, both the jubilant and the rebuffed ones, in student services around the country are the counsellors and other support services who know the reality of the experience ahead, know that the summer's promise may not be met and, more sadly, know that many students are not equipped for the emotional demands of university. It would be simplistic and insulting to say that gaining a university place is merely evidence of the capacity to pass exams and to have a head of school or year who can write a convincing reference (with an eye on league tables no doubt), since those are the grounds on which offers are made for the majority of courses and universities. Equally, it would be grandiose to say that succeeding at university is evidence of the capacity to mature through living with one's self, one's anxieties, other people and the demands of performance. It would be temperate to say that a good intellect is necessary but not sufficient to carry a student through university to a happy ending, but the intemperate statements may be useful in conveying the drama and the shock of moving from one learning institution to another, from one world to another, in the space of a few weeks.

This book is about the drama and the shock, internal and external, and it aims to reveal why university may be the worst time of life and may not lead to a prosperous career or fulfilling relationships. Based on years of work in an established counselling service, it is an informed and sympathetic account of the internal world of students as they navigate the university experience. It is sophisticated enough to be valuable to other counsellors; it is transparent enough to be beneficial to students, their families and their teachers.

Further education is rightly geared toward the future and toward maturity. Freud said that the signs of maturity are the capacity to work and to form a satisfactory intimate relationship with another person. These are major aspects of forming a personal identity and are the primary tasks of late adolescence. Further education, however, is equally a testing ground of the history of the student. Winnicott (1971) said that adolescence is the time when all the problems and successes of earlier life come home to roost. Problems will need to be revisited and worked through, and the university with its classrooms, social life, and transitional activities is the arena where this has to happen. Despite the problems, it is a propitious arena since it provides a second chance in an environment that can be extensively supportive.

With this in mind, the pivotal chapters, perhaps, are the third and fourth ones on separation and loss and families. Separation from family in order to achieve an independent life is necessary if the young person is to remain at university at all, never mind succeed at the tasks of learning and living there. Ravi Rana couples the attraction of life beyond home with the recognition of the loss entailed, and she outlines the mourning process. Just as in actual death, the person usually most needed to help the bereaved bear the loss is the one just lost; so with new students at the threshold of university, the familiarity and reliability of the family and old school community are most needed to help withstand the uncertainty and anxiety of personal budgets, strangers, sexuality, unaccustomed freedom, laundromats, libraries, laboratories, low-structured academic timetables and Freshers Fairs – and they are precisely what must be eschewed. And yet, in order for the young person to leave home, the family has to be frusrtating enough to provide the impetus to get out and lead a separate life. This paradox can give rise to unbearable conflicts, a range of which is chronicled in the vivid case studies. A student suffering the sheer loneliness of homesickness or the alienation of having chosen the wrong course may, nonetheless, seem to crowd out the counsellor's office as the whole family feels palpably present in the room. Teasing out the family dynamics and the fine line between ties that bind and bonds that tether family members together may make the difference between the student staying or going.

The nature of family relationships is set out in the first two chapters. The book opens with a thorough introduction to the psychodynamic concepts that inform the author's theory and practice. This establishes the unconscious – unconscious anxieties, conflicts and intentions – as a major player in the problems experienced by students. The second chapter on relationships tracks the expanding world of the individual from the primary relationship with the mother to encompass gradually the father, siblings, peer and social institutions. The successes and pleasures, anxieties, losses and compensations of each state are noted and illustrated. It also addresses the link between developmental and defensive processes. Failures or difficulties at any point along the developmental continuum are the problems that come to roost later as the adolescent reworks issues around separation, sexuality and identity. This may not be original text for many professionals but it is eminently readable and marvellously comprehensible for those new to thinking about intrapsychic processes. The dictionary of defences in the third chapter is an excellent reference point and demonstrates the 'paradox of irrationality' so well. The case vignettes show how we frequently end up doing precisely and disastrously the thing that we didn't want to do, thanks to our unconscious mechanisms. This is rocky terrain, but Dr Rana treads it with the sure-footed confidence of experience, so that the most apparently wacky internal situation can be grasped and appreciated.

For the proverbial reader of the medical textbook looking for him or herself in the symptom clusters, the sixth chapter about learning and study difficulties must be very welcome. In explicating the crucial link between emotional issues and intellectual problems, Dr Rana shows how blocks and disturbance in thinking, writing, concentrating, motivation, creativity, exams, classroom performance, and managing feedback (marks) – indeed, in any aspect of the academic task or subject choice – can be traced to anxieties about hunger and sexuality and to snarled relationships with parents and siblings (authority and competitors). Aside from the importance of the content of this chapter, the added value is in Dr

Rana's sympathetic and generous attitude to these ordinary and prevalent student problems. These are the kinds of difficulties that irritate and frustrate everyone – students, parents, teachers, friends – because it often seems so senseless that anyone (especially anyone as bright as an university student) would want to sabotage the opportunities of learning in these ways. Unfortunately many people will also find themselves in the next chapter on serious breakdown, self-harm and suicide. The distinction made between destructive actions directed to the self and to others is very helpful as is the attention to the anxiety and distress created in others by these painful and frightening episodes. The directness of the writing should go some way toward dispelling the conspiracy of silence around self-harm determined by fear of making it worse or bringing it on.

The final chapter on the university context pays attention to the impact of the particular features of the academic calendar and cycles on students and on the treatment options open to them if they succumb to the seasonal pressures. This chapter also draws attention to the interplay of external reality and internal dynamics. While the book is predominantly about the internal world of the student, the importance of reality has been present and taken into account all along in reference to issues such as changes in funding arrangements, in the structure of the contemporary family, and in the purposes of higher education.

At the end of the book, the reader will have learned a great deal about the vicissitudes and pleasures of university life. I hope, too, the reader will have picked up what might be called the moral of the story. Over and over again, Dr Rana indicates that difficulties can be resolved and overcome if only it is possible to stop and think. It may be asking a lot of the vulnerable or distressed adolescent (or indeed the parent at wit's end) to forgo the natural impulse to act precipitously and instead tolerate the pain of anxiety and conflict long enough to understand it. But if they can, they may not have to run home in a moment of homesickness, or ditch a relationship when it hurts, or sacrifice a degree because the exam room is to frighteningly lonely. Speaking finally to counsellors, Dr Rana also stresses the importance for counsellors of not panicking in response to the pressure of business and the often swamping anxiety of the opening moment of a counselling relationship. Students coming for help need the calm attention of a counsellor to enable them to distinguish between an emotional tidal wave and a developmental surge. This is also a message to the institution which would like quick results in the form of the student back on track for the best degree. Although the case studies in the book are short and concise, the process of counselling takes time and patience. Nor will reading this book substitute for a therapeutic relationship, but the clarity and optimism of the text may give students in trouble the confidence to seek help rather than suffer and fail.

ELLEN NOONAN

Head of Counselling Section
Faculty for Continuing Education
Birkbeck College
University of London

ACKNOWLEDGEMENTS

First and foremost I would like to thank the many students with whom I have had the privilege and pleasure of working; they have provided both the inspiration and the foundations for this book. My grateful thanks also go to my colleagues and friends for their generous and unstinting support and encouragement. In particular I wish to mention Maurice Greenberg, Faith Miles and Jacyntha Etienne who, in different ways, gave invaluable help throughout the writing of this book. Finally, I would like to thank my husband, Eric Karas, whose intellectual contribution, trenchant criticism and creative suggestions have made this a better book than it could otherwise have been.

RAVI RANA

INTRODUCTION

In writing this book, my primary aim has been to provide individuals who have a professional or personal interest in student welfare with an introduction to the main psychological and developmental factors that affect students and how these typically influence and shape their experiences at university. The opening chapters introduce the main theoretical concepts used in the book. These are explained clearly and simply with illustrative case material and are designed to be accessible to the lay reader. The following chapters examine the various emotional and developmental issues that underlie the problems most frequently experienced by students. As in the earlier chapters, I have made extensive use of case material to facilitate recognition and understanding of the issues under discussion.

The model of student counselling that I present in this book is essentially psychodynamic and derives many of its key concepts from the field of psychoanalysis. Many psychoanalytic concepts have extremely elastic definitions and the way in which I will use them here will therefore require clarification. In order to illuminate these concepts, as well as to illustrate their practical relevance, I will present examples throughout the book of the types of problems that students commonly experience, and how these might be addressed in counselling. While the various examples described are distilled from my own experience of counselling students, they are fictional in that they do not describe real students or actual events. Also, while many of the examples provided have an apparent simplicity which does not reflect the actual complexity of events in the real life situation, I think that the greater clarity obtained through such simplification makes for easier understanding of the particular issues under discussion.

Chapter 1 introduces the principal psychoanalytic concepts used in this book by taking the reader through part of a counselling session, discussing central concepts and the way in which I have understood them as they arose in the course of the session. Additional examples are presented to illustrate more fully the theoretical ideas under discussion. (At the end of each chapter there is a short list of references for readers who are interested in pursuing in greater depth some of the ideas discussed in the chapter.)

A particular feature of counselling work with students, most of whom are reaching the end of their adolescence, is the centrality of change in the life of the adolescent. In order to understand the impact of the changes, both internal and external, peculiar to this stage of development such as leaving home, moving from school to college or university, sexual relationships and so on, it is necessary to have a model of individual development which describes how changes in internal and external circumstances are negotiated and how personal and sexual identities are eventually established. In Chapter 2 I present a view of individual development which provides a context within which adaptation to change can be discussed and assessed.

For some students, higher education is firmly linked with a desire for independence and a wish to flee the parental nest, while for others a further period of study can present a means of remaining at home and avoiding the responsibility of independence. Most students fall somewhere between these two extremes and alternate between a wish to stand on their own two feet and a continuing desire to be looked after. Independence is only achieved through relinquishing more dependent aspects of the self, a process which involves loss and may evoke complex feelings. Of course the overall impact of these feelings on the individual s emotional state will depend on compensations gained through becoming more independent. For example, the establishment of close supportive relationships with flat-mates may be both immensely rewarding as well as a source of potential conflict with family who may feel excluded. While many of their contemporaries might be entering directly into the adult world of jobs and families, students occupy a sort of halfway house. Most students remain financially dependent on their parents to some extent and the vast majority are dependent on grant awarding bodies for the bulk of their tuition fees. While most students will be managing their personal finances by the time they arrive at university, few will have much experience in such areas as paying household bills. Such responsibilities may be kept at bay for a little longer by students who continue to live at home or who move into accommodation provided by the university. Separation from home is clearly a central task for most students and the emotional issues involved are examined in Chapter 3.

Whether or not they continue to live at home with their families, many students are caught up, more or less consciously, with worries or concerns about members of their family, very often their parents. For example, it is not unusual for parents who have stayed together 'for the sake of the children' to feel free to separate once their children have gone to university. For some students the dissolution of their family, and perhaps also the loss of the family home just as they are about to make their own break from home, can be felt as catastrophic. Sometimes, however, it may be the case that the family cannot cope with the departure of one of its members to university. For example, it is not uncommon for mothers who are otherwise supportive and encouraging of their child's desire for further education to become depressed when their children finally leave home to study. This reaction to their departure can be very distressing for the new student and is sometimes the underlying reason for failure to settle in at university or for early drop-out. In addition to difficulties precipitated by changes in the student's immediate family structure, problems at home such as a serious illness can drastically affect the student's ability to concentrate on their studies. In Chapter 4 the various ways in which problems at home can affect students while they are at university are explored.

It is impossible to think about student life without thinking about sex and relationships; and indeed concerns arising out of both of these areas preoccupy most students at some time or other. The construction of a secure personal identity that will support the student's emotional life is one of the central tasks of adolescence and is crucial to the development of satisfying relationships with others; 'identity crises' and the search for meaning and structure in their lives are commonly encountered during this stage. For some students the issue of their sexual identity may be problematic, perhaps because they are uncertain and confused about it or, if they are gay, because they are afraid of other people's reactions. Difficulties in establishing satisfactory relationships can be another source of distress especially if other students are seen to be managing this successfully. The breakdown of relationships, and the accompanying pain and confusion, is one of the more common reasons for students to seek the help of a counsellor. In Chapter 5 I examine the process by which a sense of personal identity is formed during adolescence; some of the factors affecting the capacity of the student for developing relationships will also be discussed.

The defining characteristic of students as a group is that they all are engaged in a protracted period of further academic study.

Chapter 6 explores the potential benefits and drawbacks for coun-selling of this emphasis on intellectual understanding. In addition some of the issues underlying typical study problems, such as work blocks and exam terrors, will be considered. Finally I present some thoughts about the underlying emotional factors that influence students in their choice of subject area at university.

Late adolescence is a turbulent period and most parents with adolescents will be familiar with the rapid mood swings and appar-ent changes in personality that accompany this period of develop-ment. The vast majority of adolescents, and their parents, weather this stormy period without too much disruption. For some individ-uals, however, the demands of adolescence prove overwhelming and a psychological breakdown occurs. If this is a temporary state, and transitory 'psychotic' episodes are not unusual among adoles-cents, the outlook is generally favourable. If not, then a psychiatric intervention is usually necessary. From the point of view of those working with students, the difficulty lies in being able to distinguish between those students who, though struggling with the vicissi-tudes of adolescence, with a bit of support, will pull through and those students for whom the battle may already be lost. This distinc-tion is vital, yet it is often not an easy one to make. Related to this issue is that of suicide and self-injury. Thoughts about death and suicide are not uncommon among adolescents and every year a number of students do in fact commit suicide. A central concern of any individual who is worried that a student might be contemplat-ing suicide will be to assess the actual risk of him or her carrying it out. Again this is not an easy matter even though a crucial one. Another area of concern is that of self-harming behaviour, for exam-ple superficial cutting of arms. While self-harm among students is not unusual, those in contact with students will nevertheless be in a position of having to judge the relative seriousness of this self-destructive behaviour and how to approach this with the student. Chapter 7 looks at some of the factors one might consider in trying to establish how serious a particular problem is and how one might respond.

Most counselling work with students is done within an institu-tional setting and the parameters of the institution are very impor-tant in informing what sort of counselling is appropriate for students as well as determining what is actually possible or permis-sible. For example, the long vacations between terms may affect both the feasibility and efficacy of longer term counselling for students who return to distant homes during holiday periods. In addition to constraints which may be placed by the institution on the type of counselling that can be provided, the particular developmental circumstances of the students themselves have to be taken into account. For most students the central developmental issue concerns the shift from dependence to independence. Counselling, with its implicit invitation to return to a more dependent position, runs counter to this developmental imperative and is more likely to be resisted by students. In keeping with this drive towards independence, help is often not sought until the student's own resources are overwhelmed and a crisis is reached. At this point a fast and flexible response may be demanded of counselling services. In Chapter 8, I look at how these particular constraints influence the practice of student counselling.

Finally, as with many other authors, I have struggled vainly to find a satisfactory solution to the problem of gender attribution. My attempts to get around the usage of pronouns such as 'he' or 'she' made for awkward reading that distracted from the text. I have continued, therefore, with the common convention of using the masculine gender.

1

THINKING ABOUT THE UNTHINKABLE: A PSYCHODYNAMIC MODEL

Sara, an intelligent and attractive young law student, arrived for her initial counselling session ten minutes early. When it was time for her session to begin she apologised for having come early. Tearfully, and with obvious embarrassment about her feelings, she began to describe how she felt intensely jealous of her boyfriend's ex-girlfriend. It emerged that his old girlfriend had been pestering Sara's boyfriend for some time and that while this had been going on Sara had been very supportive of her boyfriend and not at all troubled by feelings of jealousy. However, after this passed and Sara's relationship with her boyfriend deepened and they moved in together, she began to experience intense feelings of jealousy about her boyfriend's ex-girlfriend.

Asked about her family Sara recounted that her mother was a busy and successful lawyer, her father a banker and that she was the eldest of five children. The next in age to Sara was a sister some eleven months younger and this sister was mother's favourite. Her mother had told her that her sister had been dangerously ill for several weeks after her birth and that Sara had been looked after by an aunt during this time. Sara had used to be very jealous of her younger sister when they were children but got on very well with her now although she was still aware of her mother's preference for her.

While Sara was talking about her family, there was an insistent knock on the door. Another student had arrived late for what she thought was her counselling session. In order to sort out the confusion the counsellor stepped out of the consulting room for a moment. When the counsellor returned Sara looked lost and was unable to remember what she had been saying before the interruption. She was agitated and looked around her in a rather distracted way.

At this point, noticing Sara's upset and confusion, the counsellor commented on the interruption forced by the arrival of another student. She suggested that the temporary loss of the counsellor's attention might have stirred up old feelings associated with the time when Sara's sister was born and she had lost her mother's attention. Sara did not respond to this observation directly, however she looked at the counsellor and went on to talk about her extreme feelings of jealousy whenever her boyfriend left her for any length of time.

This account of part of an initial counselling interview demonstrates the assumption and use of some of the fundamental psychoanalytically based concepts and techniques which underpin this book. By examining the fragments of this counselling session over the course of this chapter it is hoped that a practical introduction to this theoretical framework will begin to take shape. Further examples will be given throughout the chapter to illustrate and expand the various mental structures and functions that emerge from our examination of this session. The aim of this chapter is to establish a *basic* psychodynamic model which can be used to discuss issues that may arise in understanding and counselling students. For the sake of clarity, much of the complexity and continuing debate surrounding the theoretical ideas discussed below has been omitted. (Readers who are interested in pursuing these ideas further will find a short reference list at the end of the chapter.)

The unconscious, repression and conflict

Let us begin at the beginning, with the first thoughts we might have about Sara, before she has even come into the counsellor's room. *Why has she come to see a counsellor?* Assuming that she has come of her own volition, we might guess that she has some sort of personal problem that she cannot deal with by herself and that she thinks talking to a counsellor might help her to sort it out. In order to resolve a problem, emotional or otherwise, we need to know something about it and the type of information we look for will depend on our particular way of understanding such problems. In order to explore this matter further, we will have to leave Sara aside for the time being and turn our attention to some important theoretical issues. The first of these concerns the *Unconscious* which we can approach through the following simple example. Peter was in his first year at university. His course work during the year had been outstanding and it was expected that he would do well in his end of term exams. Both Peter and his tutor were surprised therefore when he barely scraped a pass mark. Peter could offer no satisfactory explanation. His tutor was familiar with Peter's course work and had no doubts about Peter's understanding of his subject. On the basis that Peter's poor exam performance might be attributable to inadequate or inappropriate revision and examination techniques, he advised him to attend a study and examination skills class. However, having had a good deal of experience of students failing exams for no obviously apparent reason, the tutor also suggested that Peter should discuss the matter with a counsellor. The assumption here was that there might be some underlying cause that Peter was unaware of. In making this latter recommendation, Peter's tutor introduces us to the most fundamental of the psychoanalytic concepts that we shall need to consider, namely the unconscious.

The unconscious part of the mind, often referred to simply as 'the unconscious', can be thought of from a number of different perspectives. For the purposes of our discussion we will consider the unconscious first with respect to its *contents*, and second as a *dynamic system*. If we construe the unconscious first in terms of its contents then, in simple terms, the unconscious part of the mind can be thought of as both an original source of, as well as a repository for, those aspects of ourselves of which we remain oblivious. In this construction the unconscious can be understood as a reservoir from which pristine material may emerge *and* as a store into which painful or psychically intolerable experiences may be deposited and 'forgotten'. For example, Margaret, an outgoing and confident young woman, was pleasantly surprised when she came across a childhood friend at university. Over coffee they shared old school memories and her friend recalled the occasion when their teacher had caught Margaret cheating in a test and had called her out in front of the class where, red faced, she had been made to tell the whole class of her misdemeanour. However, despite her friend's vivid recollection of this event, Margaret could not remember it and she told her friend that she must have mixed her up with someone else. Here we can see that Margaret has no conscious memory of this painful experience from her childhood, rather it has been relegated to her unconscious. The process by which material is forced into the unconscious, as well as prevented from escaping from it, is termed

Repression. Of course, since the unconscious is by definition beyond our conscious level of awareness, its contents and functions cannot be directly known and have to be inferred through careful observation of phenomena over which we have little apparent conscious control such as dreams, slips of the tongue and so forth.

Our second perspective on the unconscious derives from a model concerning the operation of the mind, or *psyche,* and postulates three interacting systems, 'the conscious', 'the preconscious' and 'the unconscious'. The middle system, the preconscious, can be thought of as a sort of half-way house which contains elements that are out of immediate conscious awareness but that are not yet fully unconscious in the strictest sense of the word. Memories that are not currently conscious but can be relatively easily evoked would fall into this category. The important point about this model lies in the nature of the relationship between these three systems. Basically, it is assumed that the unconscious is a *dynamic* system, by which is meant that it continually seeks conscious expression, and that this imperative brings it into *Conflict* with the preconscious system which is opposed to the emergence of raw material from the unconscious. The task of the preconscious is to censor and filter the unconscious material allowing it into consciousness in a psychically tolerable form. Through this process of modification a compromise between the unconscious drive and that part of the psyche which is opposed to expression is reached and it is this process that is responsible for what we call symptoms.

If we return to Sara at this point, we might surmise that feelings of jealousy bound up with *her mother's relationship with her sister* have been repressed and, through the work of the preconscious, have become attached instead to her boyfriend's relationship with his ex-girlfriend where they are now consciously available. When her counsellor turns her attention temporarily away from Sara to another student and Sara subsequently appears upset, her counsellor surmises, on the basis of what Sara has told her about her past jealousy of her sister, that the interruption of her session by the arrival of another student might have stirred up old feelings of jealousy in relation to her sister. However, when the counsellor suggests to Sara that these feelings might be related to her baby sister's arrival when she was still a baby herself, Sara does not consciously register this historical link. Instead she talks about feelings of jealousy in the context of her current relationship; the earlier connection has been repressed, probably because she was unable to manage the powerful feelings aroused in her during the time around her sister's birth.

The term 'psychodynamic' is used to describe those theoretical frameworks that assume the existence of such a dynamic unconscious and recognise that it constantly exerts an enormous and crucial influence over our conscious thoughts and actions. In other words, this means that much of what we feel, think and do is not under our direct conscious control but is determined by mental processes of which we are mostly unaware. The position of the preconscious is a little more complicated. Descriptively speaking, the preconscious is unconscious in the sense that it lies outside of immediate awareness, however, the operational characteristics of the preconscious system are closer to those of the conscious system (as discussed below) and, for the purposes of this model, it can therefore be taken together with the conscious system. There is then a constant state of tension, or conflict, between the unconscious and the preconscious/conscious systems arising out of the unconscious' constant struggle for recognition.

The following example illustrates the powerful effect of the internal world in determining psychic reality, in this case to protect the individual from painful external realities. Janice's mother had died in a car accident a few months before she sat her A-levels. Janice appeared to have coped remarkably well with her mother's death and came to university the following year. On starting at university, however, she began to have dreams in which she and her mother would be doing things together, shopping, playing the piano, just as they had when her mother had been alive. The dreams themselves were very pleasant but Janice regularly burst into tears when she woke up. Having brought her mother to life through her dreams, it seemed that Janice then went through the very painful experience of losing her every time she woke up. In this case, we could say that during sleep Janice was using her inner world to protect herself from the painful reality of her mother's death. In this example we can clearly see the conflict between the unconscious and conscious. At a conscious level, Janice knew that her mother was dead, however in her dreams this evidence was denied and she had pleasurable emotional experiences of her mother as being alive. The conflict that existed as a result of these two incompatible levels of psychic experience was evident in Janice's distress when she woke up. While her unconscious denial of her mother's death defended her against the profoundly painful feelings that would otherwise beset her, this protection could only be sustained at the expense of her conscious awareness of her mother's death. She was unable to grieve her mother's loss because that would mean giving up her unconscious denial of it, but at the same time she was constantly reminded of the fact of it every morning when she woke up.

In the previous paragraph, 'the operational characteristics' of the preconscious system were mentioned as being similar to those of the conscious system and distinct from those of the unconscious system. The essential difference between the 'laws' governing the preconscious/conscious systems and the unconscious system lies in their relation to the external world. Thus, the preconscious/conscious systems are ruled by the ordinary precepts of time and space that structure the real world. The unconscious, by contrast, has no direct link with the external world and does not recognise its authority. This idea might seem more familiar if we think about our dreams in which the ordinary constraints of the real world are often absent, for example, one particularly harassed student reported a dream in which she was flying free as a bird, which is of course a gross violation of the laws of gravity. We can also use our experience of dreams to illustrate another important point about the unconscious, namely the distinction between *psychic reality* and *external reality*. Put crudely, psychic reality describes our inner or subjective apprehension of the world while external or material reality refers to the world as it actually is. Ordinarily, psychic reality and external reality inform one another and a relatively comfortable balance prevails. However this equilibrium can be easily disturbed, and indeed is routinely upset every night when we go to sleep. For example, when Martin woke up screaming that his hair was on fire, he still needed to touch his head to convince himself that he had only been dreaming. In order to sleep we generally need to make a substantial reduction in our conscious awareness of external stimuli, we close the curtains, shut our eyes, and turn down the sound. However this temporary daily withdrawal from the external world inevitably causes a shift in emphasis in favour of our internal world with the result that unconscious influences dominate psychic reality in a more apparent way. This accounts both for the apparently bizarre nature of dreams as well as for their experientially real quality. In our example, Martin needed to reacquaint himself with material reality in order to mitigate the terrifying feelings arising from his psychic reality.

At first glance it may appear that the unconscious only harbours negative and destructive aspects of ourselves, and that this is the reason for the conscious mind's repudiation of it. This is not so, potentially constructive forces may also be held back in the unconscious. The primary concern of the preconscious system is to avoid conflict, as illustrated in the following two examples. The first student, Mary, is unable to acknowledge and deploy her competitive impulses constructively to promote her creativity while the second student, Jeremy, unconsciously deprives himself of his intellectual abilities in order to pre-empt any awareness of his hugely conflictual feelings towards his mother.

Mary's tutor was surprised when she refused to enter an essay competition at her university. Mary enjoyed writing, her essays had always been excellent and her tutor believed that she stood a very good chance of winning. On top of this, her tutor knew that Mary came from a large family and that money was tight and that she could well use the substantial prize money. Mary's best friend, who was also hard up, had submitted her own essay for the competition, however when she had encouraged Mary to enter too, Mary had said that she couldn't be bothered. In this case, Mary's wish to enter the competition and win the prize money could not be allowed conscious access because it stirred up anxiety about competing with, and possibly beating, her best friend. This anxiety had its roots in childhood experiences of having to compete with her brothers and sisters for scarce family resources. Here the potential conflict between Mary's unconscious desire to satisfy herself without taking account of the effect on her best friend and her concern about her relationship with her friend is resolved by Mary's disavowal of any desire to compete. Thus Mary's unconscious anxieties about competing interfere with her capacity to use her talents productively, in this case to improve her financial circumstances.

Our second example demonstrates the disastrous effects of unconscious hostile feelings in one student's life. Jeremy, an intelligent young man who had never been able to acknowledge to himself how furious his doting mother's demands for success made him feel, had been very upset when he failed his final year exams. However, by depriving his mother of what she wanted, namely a successful son, he had been able to satisfy his repressed or unconscious rage at his mother without having to become aware of his feelings of hostility towards her. Thus, by sacrificing his university degree he was able to remain oblivious to the conflict within himself which was to do with his anger at his mother's demandingness and his fear of the consequences for their relationship were he to became aware of his hostile feelings towards her.

Despite the ubiquity of the experience that we are not entirely conscious masters of our own fate, the realisation of this fact never ceases to surprise us, as evident in comments like, 'Why on earth did I do that ... I don't know what came over me ... etc.' One corollary of our difficulty in believing in an unconscious area of mind in ourselves is a disbelief in the possibility of its existence in others. Thus, when a student who has been struggling hard to concentrate on his work complains to his father that he has a 'mental block', and his worried father exhorts him to try harder, we see clearly the father's belief that his son's mind is completely under his conscious control and that he could work if he really wanted to. The notion that a student's inability to concentrate might have its origins outside of his conscious awareness, and by implication outside of his conscious control, is a difficult idea for many people to embrace, be they parents, tutors or fellow students. The following example illustrates one student's perplexity. Seema was at a loss as to why she couldn't concentrate on her law books. She had had no problems in keeping her mind on her studies during her A-levels and her current difficulties baffled her. When asked if she liked her law course, she had replied that it hadn't been her first choice and that she had wanted to study music. However, her parents had said that she wouldn't be able to make a living out of music and she guessed they were probably right. Here we can see that Seema's renunciation of her own wishes in favour of the more practical advice of her parents has failed to resolve the conflict between her desire to please her parents and her wish to follow her own interests, at this time music, at the risk of rejecting her parents' advice. Under the circumstances, her difficulty in concentrating on her law books might also be an expression of her unconscious wish to turn away from, or rebel against, her parents' wishes.

We can now return to Sara and to our original question as to why she has come to see a counsellor. On the basis of our discussion above, it might be reasonable to assume that Sara has some problem that she is unable to sort out for herself because its determinants are unconscious and therefore not available for her to think about. It follows therefore that Sara will be unable to tell the counsellor directly what her unconscious concerns are even though these may be crucial to an understanding of her inability to solve her current problem. The counsellor's task is therefore to notice and hopefully make sense of precisely those things which Sara cannot as yet know for herself about herself. In this task the counsellor has an invaluable aid in a ubiquitous feature of human relationships, namely the phenomenon of 'transference' which we will now discuss.

Transference and countertransference

Sara's need for help and her inability to sort out her problem herself inevitably place her in a position of dependence in relation to the counsellor. How Sara will feel about asking for help will, to a considerable extent, depend on her previous experience of such situations. Individuals vary greatly in the ease with which they are able to reveal their own weaknesses and needs to others as well as in their capacity to ask for help. The problems of one first year mathematics student, Michael, only came to light when a tutor, who had reached the end of his patience on failing to receive any assignments from Michael after two terms, finally went to visit him at his halls of residence. Unable to get started on his work, Michael had gradually fallen further and further behind with his work and, despairing of ever catching up, he had given up attending his classes altogether. Michael's reticence in seeking help was in marked contrast to Maria's. In the week before she started at university Maria went to see a counsellor. She was afraid she wouldn't fit in or make any friends and was desperately looking for encouragement and support. Why should Michael be so reluctant to seek out help and Maria so eager? One way of looking at this might be in terms of their different expectations of finding help. Michael, for example, was afraid that his tutor would be unsympathetic to his plight and, like his father, get angry and impatient with him for his difficulty in settling down to his work. Maria, however, who was accustomed to her mother anxiously phoning her every evening to check that she was all right, expected that the counsellor would want to see her regularly for up to date reports on her latest worries. What is immediately apparent is that both Michael and Maria had a predetermined idea about how the person they approached with their problems would respond to them, and also that their expectations were loosely based on their past experiences with their parents. This phenomenon, in which past experiences unconsciously influence present expectations of relationships, is termed *Transference*. There is considerable debate as to whether the concept of transference should be used restrictively to describe phenomena peculiar to the therapeutic relationship or whether it should be applied more widely to all relationships. The position that will be taken here is that transference is a universal feature of all relationships but that the therapeutic relationship is especially refined in order to foster and explore transference phenomena. Essentially, transference refers to a psychological process in which attitudes and feelings originally attached to an important figure in the past, often a parent, are (re-) experienced in relation to someone in the present. The important point here is that these feelings are felt as arising out of the current relationship and their connection with past figures is not recognised. This was clearly the case with Sara, whose extreme feelings of jealousy of her younger sister's intimacy with their mother were 'transferred' onto her relationship with her boyfriend. It will be evident that this tendency to view the present through lenses ground out of past experience will also affect the student's perception of the counsellor and will inevitably influence his feelings and behaviour towards the counsellor. The extent to which current perceptions are distorted in this way, or to put it another way the intensity of the transference, will depend on a number of factors, including the congruence of the past and present situations. Again, Sara's obvious disturbance following the interruption of her session with the counsellor by another student demanding her counsellor's attention suggested an already strong transferential element in her relationship with the counsellor.

The following example illustrates the powerful effect of transference in shaping another student's behaviour in relation to her counsellor. Sonia had been bulimic for several years. She had a younger brother whom she spoke about with some irritation. Unlike Sonia who had excelled at school and gone away to university, her brother had left school with poor A-level grades and was unemployed and living at home. A combination of minor health problems and indifference to school work had resulted in her brother often staying home and missing school. Sonia recounted how her mother constantly complained to her about her brother's passivity and dependence on her but, in Sonia's eyes, her mother did nothing to discourage him. By contrast, her mother said that Sonia had never given her any trouble. Sonia was offered five counselling sessions which she gratefully accepted. Over the course of the first three sessions she appeared to gain a great deal of understanding and she was eager and willing to face up to a lot of difficult and potentially painful observations about herself. She appeared to be in many ways an ideal student to counsel. Sonia felt that she was learning a great deal about herself and she considered that a very good start, after all, she said, she didn't expect miracles. In the penultimate session, however, there was a marked change in her mood. She expressed pessimism about relationships ever lasting and confided her belief that she would end up with a series of divorces. She thought that she would never be able to find someone who would

be able to give her what she wanted. In response to this the counsellor raised the issue of Sonia's impending ending with her and her
feelings about that. Sonia said that she had felt a little bit angry but
realised that, 'oh well . . . nothing ever lasts'. The counsellor went on
to suggest that Sonia might find longer-term therapy helpful. When
Sonia returned for her final session she told the counsellor that she
had been angry and upset after leaving the last session. She had
thought that it was unfair that things didn't last and she had felt like
bingeing. However, on this occasion she had been able to resist the
temptation to binge which her counsellor understood in terms of
Sonia's ability to experience her anger and disappointment rather
than express it via a binge.

In this example, we can see an important facet of Sonia's relationship with her mother unfolding in the transference relationship
with the counsellor. Sonia behaves towards her mother as though
her mother's positive regard for her is contingent upon her being
'no trouble'. She makes few demands upon her mother and strives
to be self-sufficient. Indeed we might say that she mothers her
mother by listening to her endless complaints about her brother.
Sonia's attitude towards her mother is readily apparent in the transference, initially in her failure to express her anxiety about the
brevity of the counselling contract offered to her and in her diligent
application to the task of understanding herself. She is determined
to look after herself and to make as few demands as possible upon
the counsellor. She even looks after the counsellor by letting her
know how well things are going. At the same time, however, in her
family she harbours feelings of irritation towards both her brother
and her mother. She feels annoyed with her brother for making what
appear to her to be inordinate demands upon her mother *and* she
feels angry with her mother for giving in to her brother. This
suggests that Sonia is ambivalent about her own needs in relation to
her mother. Although she feels angry that her mother satisfies her
brother's demands, she is unwilling to admit to any such needs in
herself and so fails to obtain anything satisfying for herself from her
mother. In her penultimate counselling session, her anger and disappointment break through but she is still minimising of her own
needs. However, the counsellor recognises and supports Sonia's
indirectly stated need for more substantial help and this enables her
to acknowledge some of her feelings in relation to the counsellor,
albeit after the session has ended.

Returning briefly to Sara, we might have noticed that she was in
fact ten minutes early for her appointment. At this stage it is

impossible to determine the significance, if any, of Sara's early arrival and we will therefore leave it to one side for the time being. (As we will see later, Sara's early arrival was salient to our understanding of her problems.) It will have become clear by now that even before Sara sets foot in the counsellor's room, she is likely to have all sorts of thoughts and feelings about the coming meeting and that she will already have unconscious expectations in relation to the counsellor, in other words, the process of transference will be well under way. However, before we look at what transpires when Sara does finally come into the counsellor's room, there is a further related phenomenon that must be considered, namely *Countertransference*. For our purposes, countertransference can be thought of as referring to those thoughts and feelings, conscious as well as unconscious, that are aroused in the counsellor *in response to* some communication, which may be conscious or unconscious, from the student. The following example illustrates this phenomenon. David had originally sought help because he had fallen behind with his assignments. His mother had been diagnosed as having breast cancer some months earlier and he had been unable to concentrate on his work since then. His father had reassured him that his mother would be fine and that he needn't worry and should get on with his studies. David said that he had accepted his father's assurances but was still unable to apply himself to his work and he was full of self-reproach for this. He added that his father was not the sort to talk about feelings and that he usually talked to his mother when he was worried about something but obviously he could not do that now. Wondering whether David might not have experienced his father's attitude towards his anxieties as somewhat dismissive, the counsellor asked him how he felt about his father's response to his concerns. He said that he felt fine about it and repeated that his father had never been one to talk about feelings. He then returned to his worries about his work. Meanwhile, David's counsellor had noticed that, in spite of her sympathy for his painful situation at home, she had nevertheless begun to feel irritated with him. Reflecting on her anger and David's apparent reluctance to think about his feelings about his father, the counsellor surmised that her feelings of anger in fact 'belonged' to David and were probably related to David's unconscious angry feelings towards his father for glossing over his worries about his mother. While it was not fully clear why David could not simply express his frustration with his father directly to him, it seemed likely that, at an unconscious level, he was afraid of a rejecting or hostile response from his father, who had made it plain that he did not like to talk about emotional issues, and was protecting himself from such a painful outcome by repressing his feelings of anger towards his father. In this example, then, we can see how the counsellor's feelings of anger were directly related to David's unconscious feelings of anger towards his father. We could say that David had unconsciously communicated his unconscious feelings of anger in relation to his father to his counsellor and that this was the source of the counsellor's countertransference feelings of anger. This formulation of David's counsellor's countertransference feelings of course presupposes that the counsellor does not harbour negative feelings of his own, conscious or otherwise, towards David. (The psychological processes underlying transference and countertransference phenomena will be discussed in Chapter 2.)

The distinction between countertransference feelings, which have their source *in the student*, and thoughts and feelings which have their origins *in the counsellor* is an important one though not always an easy one to make. For example, Emily's counsellor was aware of feeling protective towards Emily and of having to resist an impulse to give her helpful little tips, like the best place to go to find second hand books for her course. Emily was in her first year and had come to study in a big city university from a small fishing village. She was somewhat shy and apprehensive but was slowly finding her feet and her initial feelings of isolation had begun to dissolve as she found friends among her classmates. Her counsellor could appreciate that Emily was settling in well but nonetheless she continued to feel worried for her. Reflecting on the disparity between her level of concern for Emily and Emily's actual anxieties, she thought about her own experience many years earlier when she too had left a small community to study in a big town. She recalled how lonely she had felt and how she had longed for someone to offer a helping hand. Thus, in trying to look after Emily, the counsellor was responding to unfulfilled and 'forgotten' longings stirred up in her by this student who literally put her in mind of her younger self.

It will hopefully be plain from the examples given above that transference and countertransference phenomena are an inevitable and universal feature of all human relationships. It is well nigh impossible to enter into any interaction without some preconceptions, though of course the extent to which these affect our experience of others varies enormously. The following everyday example illustrates the relative malleability of our perception of situations.

Mark and Sophie are classmates. Mark lacks confidence in his academic abilities and when his lecturer asks how he's getting along Mark worries that the lecturer thinks he's not up to the course and is checking up on him. Sophie on the other hand is enjoying her course and when the lecturer enquires about how things are going, she is pleased at this opportunity to talk about her work. Thus Mark and Sophie's emotional responses to essentially the same question are very different, Mark feels threatened by the lecturer while Sophie feels flattered by his interest. The ubiquity of transference and countertransference processes make them invaluable guides to unconscious feelings and, as we shall see, can be of enormous help in illuminating otherwise obscure areas of the unconscious.

Anxiety

Let us return to Sara. Sara has now come into the counsellor's room. She appears nervous and her first comment is to apologise for having arrived *early*. This apparently straightforward communication is nonetheless interesting and affords some initial insight into Sara's unconscious psychological processes. Despite being in a state of considerable distress herself and understandably eager for help, her first concern on meeting the counsellor is to apologise for some imagined inconvenience she has put her to by arriving some minutes before her appointment time. Before we explore the possible reasons for Sara's anxiety, we will clarify what we mean by anxiety here. *Anxiety* can be thought of as an emotional state which is accompanied by a number of unpleasant physical sensations and which generally occurs in anticipation of a painful or dangerous situation. The threat may be external, arising in the world out there or internal and a product of our minds. More often anxiety is a response to some mixture of the two. For example, anxiety before examinations is commonplace among students and, if it doesn't become too intense, is an important source of motivation for many students. However, high levels of anxiety can be disabling as in the following two examples. Jenny had worked hard all year and, being well prepared, she was not unduly worried about her forthcoming examinations. On the first morning of her finals there was an accident on the railway line that she took to university. The train she had planned to get was cancelled and it was uncertain whether the next train, which would get her there a few minutes late, would be running. Her anxiety, in this case in response to an *external* threat, escalated and she felt panicky and sick. Fortunately, the second train did run and she reached the examination hall only a few minutes late. However, her fear of missing the exam had so unsettled her that she was unable to think and it was some time before she recovered her composure sufficiently to make a start on the exam papers. Simon had also worked hard all year and in this respect was well prepared for his first examinations but, whereas Jenny expected to pass her exams, as the examinations approached Simon became increasingly anxious, fearing that he would be unable to answer any of the exam questions.' In the examination hall, he barely looked at the exam paper before he got up and left. An invigilator stopped him and asked if he was sure about leaving to which he replied that there was no point in staying since his mind had gone completely blank. Simon subsequently went for counselling during the course of which the *internal* origins of his anxiety became apparent. It emerged that Simon had always felt himself to be in the shadow of his older and more successful brother and, while his parents never made any overt comparisons between them, he had felt that his brother was the favoured of the two. Within this context, Simon's anxieties about his performance during his exams might be understood, in part at least, in terms of his competitiveness with his brother, of which he was only dimly aware, and the intense feelings of failure and inadequacy that this appeared to arouse in him. Whatever the cause of Simon's anxiety, its destructive effect on his capacity to think was abundantly clear. Simon denied any parental pressure to succeed, but many students are aware of some pressure from their families which, combined with their own more or less conscious expectations of themselves, inevitably provokes some anxiety about examinations. Here the origins of their anxiety stem from a mixture of internal and external concerns. Often, where the source of anxiety is internal, the individual may experience anxiety without being aware of its origins, as was the case with Simon.

We are now in a position to consider Sara's encounter with her counsellor in greater depth. Sara's initial anxiety seems to relate to the counsellor and seems to be about being a nuisance. Sara appears to believe that the urgency of her needs, betrayed through her early arrival, will be experienced by the counsellor as unwelcome. Without waiting for any confirmation, Sara acts upon her expectation that the counsellor will be displeased with her and defends herself by apologising. It is clear that Sara's anxiety at this point is internal, in other words, that she is defending herself from a self-generated threat even though she feels it to be coming from a source external to herself, that is, from the counsellor whom she fears will be angry with her for her demandingness. At the same time, at a deeper unconscious level, it may be that it is Sara herself who feels angry because the counsellor has kept her waiting despite her obvious distress. However to acknowledge such unreasonable feelings in herself might disturb her perception of herself as a mature young woman who can manage to wait ten minutes for an appointment. *If* this construction is accurate, then we might think that Sara has an unconscious conflict between her anger at being kept waiting and her fear of upsetting the counsellor and jeopardising any possible help the counsellor might have to offer. In this case, Sara's anxiety is that her potential fury at being kept waiting will break through and will damage her nascent relationship with the counsellor whose help she is seeking. This is not dissimilar to the dilemma Jeremy faced in relation to his mother's demandingness when he had to find a way of satisfying the conflicting demands of his unconscious destructive feelings towards his mother and his conscious wish to preserve their relationship. So how does Sara deal with her particular conflict and the accompanying anxiety? It would appear that initially she adopts the same strategy as Jeremy, that is, she keeps any potential hostile feelings towards the counsellor firmly beyond her conscious awareness. However, while Jeremy vented his unconscious hostile feelings by turning them against himself and failing his degree, Sara responds as though she had *already* displeased the counsellor in some way. These psychological manoeuvres, which are triggered by anxiety, are designed to protect the individual from becoming aware of unconscious and potentially painful conflicts. Such mechanisms, termed 'defences', are the ways in which the mind protects itself from the exigencies of the unconscious part of the mind, generally through some sort of compromise. As indicated earlier, conflict within the unconscious, or between the unconscious and conscious parts of the mind is a normal state of affairs and the establishment of defences to deal with these warring factions is both necessary and adaptive. For the most part both our conflicts and our defences remain unconscious and do not cause concern, however, as in any dynamic system, forces can become unbalanced and under such circumstances, defences can give rise to more problems than they solve as we saw in Jeremy's case. Much of the work in counselling students revolves around the clarification and exploration of defences that are inappropriate, like Sara's, or are not working adequately or effectively and we will look at this area in more detail in Chapter 3.

Having dealt with her pressing and unwanted feelings of anger towards her counsellor, Sara is now free to talk about her problem. However, her evident shame as she describes her feelings of jealousy towards her boyfriend's ex-girlfriend suggests that it is not only feelings of anger that she finds unacceptable. Sara expresses surprise that her jealous feelings have waxed and not waned as she expected they would with her boyfriend's increasing commitment to their relationship. Noting that Sara's problem appeared to be exacerbated by a deepening of feelings between her and her boyfriend, and putting this together with her own recent experience of Sara's need to get rid of unwanted feelings, the counsellor surmises that Sara may now be struggling against recognising other unacceptable feelings which have arisen in relation to her flourishing attachment to her boyfriend. In other words, the counsellor is beginning to think that Sara's problem may be to do with ambivalent feelings that are stirred up in her when she becomes emotionally close to someone.

In order to find out more about how Sara has managed other important emotional attachments in her life, the counsellor asks her about her family. Early family experiences are crucial in structuring the patterns of later relationships and information pertaining to early relationships is therefore often illuminating. (The importance of early family relations in the development of the individual will be discussed in more detail in Chapter 2.)

In response to the counsellor's inquiry, Sara gives some interesting information about her family. In particular the counsellor notices that Sara's mother has a demanding job as well as five children to attend to, of whom Sara is the eldest. She also notes that Sara has in fact suffered from intense feelings of jealousy earlier in her life in relation to the sister who came directly after her. In addition, the counsellor discovers that while Sara continues to be aware that her sister is still her mother's favourite, she does not feel jealous of her any longer and finally, that Sara has chosen to follow her mother's career.

Remembering through repeating

At this stage the counsellor is able to see a common thread connecting Sara's current problems in relation to her boyfriend and her previous jealousy of her sister. In both cases, Sara experiences intense feelings of jealousy when someone comes between her and the person she is close to. In the past she became intensely jealous of her baby sister who came between her and her mother when she was still a little baby herself, and now she feels jealous of anyone who might vie with her for her boyfriend's affections. Thus, while she and her boyfriend were actively united in fending off his ex-girlfriend's advances, Sara's potential feelings of jealousy were kept at bay. However, once this external threat that she could consciously confront had passed, she was assailed by internally fuelled anxieties about someone coming between her and her boyfriend and, in particular, she feared his ex-girlfriend who had, after all, been the object of his affections long before herself. Given she had felt usurped in her mother's affections by her younger sister, her anxiety in this regard was not unexpected. Bearing in mind that Sara is no longer aware of any feelings of jealousy towards her sister, we might suppose that Sara has dealt with these painful feelings about losing her mother's attention to her younger sister by repression and that it is these unconscious feelings that have been revitalised in her current relationship with her boyfriend. In other words, her unconscious fear of losing the person she loved, originally her mother, to someone else is 'remembered' through the process of being 'repeated', or re-enacted, in her current relationship. The re-emergence of past, and hitherto unconscious, anxieties in current situations and relationships is commonplace yet often catches us by surprise. For example, Abigail, a successful mathematics student, was perplexed by the paralysing anxiety she experienced on the day of her driving test. She enjoyed driving and had approached her test with confidence. However, when the examiner sat in the car next to her she froze. She was sure this had never happened to her before. Then she remembered an occasion at primary school. She had been thrilled to get a starring role in the school play and could hardly wait for the day of the performance. However, when it came to her turn to step out on the stage she froze and despite her parents' encouragement from the front row, she had been unable to remember her carefully rehearsed lines and had to be helped off. She had been inconsolable and had subsequently avoided performing in front of others whenever possible. In this example, we can see how Abigail had 'forgotten' the upsetting incident at school only to 'remember' it through 'repeating' the painful experience during her driving test. Generally speaking, painful or unacceptable experiences that have been repressed require some impetus in order to reappear in the present. The individual's current situation can therefore often provide helpful clues as to the nature of the underlying anxieties. For example, Sara's outbreak of jealousy occurred in the context of a deepening attachment to her boyfriend which directed her counsellor towards an exploration of Sara's earlier family attachments. Further evidence attesting to the insecurity of Sara's attachments came via an unforeseen interruption in her counselling session.

Interpretation and the 'here-and-now'

While Sara is talking there is an insistent knock at the door and the counsellor leaves the room to attend to a student who has come at the wrong time. On her return she observes that Sara appears lost and distressed and is completely unable to pick up from where she left off. While this recent intrusion is certainly unfortunate, the counsellor is struck by the intensity of Sara's reaction to this event and she decides to make an *Interpretation* conveying her understanding of the ongoing situation to Sara. Interpretations which are based on observations of emotional events as they occur within the session are sometimes termed 'transference interpretations' because they are derived from the transference relationship. The aim of such interpretations is to expose the unconscious attitudes and feelings which underlie the emotional experience that the individual is having at that moment in the room with the counsellor. In this example, the counsellor takes the view that Sara's distress has been occasioned by her abandonment of her while she attended to another student and that the intensity of Sara's response implies that unconscious anxieties which have been stimulated by this event have become active. She therefore suggests to Sara that she has been upset by the interruption in their discussion. In this statement the counsellor is attending to Sara's immediate *Here-and-now* experience. She then goes on to make a link to Sara's past relationships and suggests that this intrusion may have triggered off childhood anxieties associated with the interruption in her relationship with her mother occasioned by her sister's arrival. Here the counsellor has made a 'transference interpretation', in other words, she has tried to understand Sara's emotional reaction to her brief abandonment of her in the session in terms of a past relationship experience. In other words, unconscious feelings relating to Sara's mother's abandonment of her were (re-)experienced by Sara in relation to her counsellor and it was this transference that the counsellor was seeking to illuminate through her interpretation.

Before turning to Sara's response, a few comments concerning the literality of the interpretation described above are necessary. It is unlikely that the intrusion by another student into Sara's session with her counsellor did in fact trigger off exactly, or even solely, feelings experienced when Sara was a baby. Given her mother's demanding job and the arrival of several other children it is more than likely that Sara often felt abandoned by her busy mother. However, this scenario of a hard pressed mother who has to leave one very young baby in order to go off and have another one is a useful metaphor and has the virtue of being consistent with Sara's own account of her family history. Also, in temporally situating Sara's 'original' experience of being left for someone else at such an early age, the counsellor was responding to the pre-verbal quality of Sara's distress when she left her.

So how does Sara respond to this interpretation of her anxiety and confusion? While she does not explicitly agree or disagree with the counsellor's intervention, she makes eye contact with her and begins to talk about her feelings. Sara's re-engagement suggests that she has felt understood by the counsellor's attempt to make sense of her recent emotional upset. Sara now goes on to talk about how extremely jealous she feels when her boyfriend leaves her for any length of time. This divulgence of feelings of jealousy *as a response to being left* by her boyfriend indicates that the counsellor's interpretation was effective and that Sara feels that the counsellor does understand how she feels. Thus, we see how an accurate interpretation can deepen rapport within the session and promote further exploration of feelings within the session.

In Chapter 2 we will explore in more depth how past experiences structure and inform our internal psychological world.

Further reading

Bateman, A. and Holmes, J. (1995) *Introduction to Psychoanalysis: Contemporary Theory and Practice*, Routledge: London and New York.

Brown, D. and Pedder, J. (1993) *Introduction to Psychotherapy: An Outline of Psychodynamic Principles and Practice*, 2nd edn, London: Routledge.

Malan, D. (1979) *Individual Psychotherapy and the Science of Psychodynamics*, London: Butterworth.

Sandler, J., Dare, C. and Holder, A. (1992) *The Patient and the Analyst*, 2nd edn, London: Karnac.

2

WHERE DO RELATIONSHIPS COME FROM? HOW WE LEARN TO RELATE

In Chapter 1, we introduced a basic psychodynamic model describing mental function. We also discussed some of the implications of this model for the practising counsellor. However, in order to appreciate the multifarious expression of mental activity in each individual, we need to take account of the particular historical context in which he or she has grown up, and for this we require a model which can describe the psychological development of the individual. In this chapter we will attempt to give an account of the *evolution and development* of the various mental structures and functions that make each individual, and their problems, unique. There are many different and valid perspectives from which personal psychological development can be viewed, for example biological models may place special emphasis on the role of genetic or physical maturational factors in the development of the individual while sociological models are more likely to focus on influences arising out of cultural and social groupings. In our discussion we will explore the development of the individual in the context of his family. In particular we will be examining how early relationships between the person and each of the family members are built up and how the vicissitudes of these relationships structure their personality and subsequent relationships outside of the family. As in Chapter 1, we will be drawing upon psychoanalytical constructs for the basis of our model.

Mother–baby relationship: splitting; projection and internalisation; containment

We will begin with a few basic facts of life, namely that each baby has a mother and a father and that, in order for a baby to survive, someone will have to take care of the baby. To put it another way, a baby starts life utterly dependent on someone else for their continuing safe existence. Typically this 'someone' is the baby's mother and in this discussion we will assume that the primary caretaker of the baby is the mother. However, it should be borne in mind that in some cultures and social situations, the role of primary caretaker may be taken by another family member, perhaps a grandmother, or an individual brought in specifically for the purpose of looking after the baby. The fact of a baby's absolute dependence on his mother makes the centrality of his relationship with her inevitable. Without her he cannot survive and her continued well-being therefore becomes a matter of immense importance to him. A baby's dependence on his mother derives from the fact that he has needs, both emotional and physical, that he cannot satisfy for himself, for example he may be hungry. We can use this simple example of a hungry baby to illustrate some aspects of how a baby's relationship with his mother is built up. We will assume that the sensation of hunger is unpleasurable and that the longer it persists the more uncomfortable the baby will feel until there comes a point when he can bear it no longer and he starts to cry. At this stage we might say that the baby is crying because of the pain he feels on account of his hunger. However, we might also observe another aspect of his experience, namely that there is nothing he can do himself to relieve his hunger. He is helpless and, in the face of his hunger, this has become a most unpleasant experience. His crying turns to screams and we might now say that he is full of rage *both* because he is hungry *and* because there is nothing he can do about it. From the baby's point of view the whole of his world – and for all intents and purposes, at this stage this means his mother – has become intolerably frustrating. His mother is denying him what he needs, namely to be fed, and his enormous anger at this situation is amply evident in his screams. At the same time, he is becoming very painfully aware of his own powerlessness. To put it another way, as long as his mother can be completely relied upon to meet his every need as it arises, his total dependence on her is untroublesome and indeed, pleasurable. In other words, as long as he can completely control his mother so that his every wish is her desire, so to speak, then he can remain happily oblivious of his dependence on her. However, every time his mother fails to anticipate or meet his needs, he will inevitably experience a degree of frustration and he will be faced with the realisation that his mother is not under his complete and utter control and that he is, after all, dependent on her. Since the baby's world consists primarily of his mother, this is a potentially catastrophic situation for him because the very person upon whom he is totally dependent is the same person who is responsible for frustrating him, sometimes terribly, from time to time. How can he both vent his feelings of frustration and anger towards his mother *and yet* save and protect her, and ultimately himself, from them? The way in which the baby deals with this dilemma, basically one of loving and hating the same person, is through a primitive unconscious psychological process termed *Splitting*. Thus the baby splits his experience of his mother into two, so that in his mind there is a 'good mother' who satisfies him and whom he loves and a 'bad mother' who frustrates him and whom he hates. By maintaining this split he endeavours to keep his good experiences from coming into contact with, and becoming damaged by, his bad experiences. For the new baby, splitting is a very necessary defence against unbearable and potentially overwhelming levels of frustration and anxiety which inevitably arise from his mother's inability to be in perfect touch with his every need. It enables the baby who is not yet able to tolerate intense and painful feelings, to protect his good experiences with his mother from being destroyed by the destructive feelings that result from his frustration with her. While splitting clearly offers a solution to the baby's immediate problem of preserving a good mother in his mind from his fury, there is a price to pay, namely recognition of reality. What the baby is avoiding by splitting is an awareness of the reality that the mother whom he hates, and in his hatred wishes to destroy, is one and the same as the mother whom he loves and wishes to preserve and he is not yet able to face this reality because of the intensity of his destructive feelings.

While splitting is ordinarily prevalent in babies and young children, adults may resort to splitting when faced with feelings that are beyond their ability to bear. For example, Fiona's counsellor had had to cancel her previous counselling session at short notice. At her next session Fiona dismissed the counsellor's apology as unnecessary and began to talk about some further problems she had been having with her end of term project. She had been struggling with this project for some weeks and, after some exploration in her counselling sessions of her unwillingness to seek her tutor's help, she had finally made an appointment to see him. However when she had turned up for her appointment the tutor's secretary had passed on the message that he was very sorry but he had had to attend an unexpected faculty meeting and that he would be happy to see her at the same time the next day. Fiona had been furious and, in a fit of pique, told the secretary that she wasn't sure if she would be able to make the alternative time offered. Later that day she complained bitterly to her counsellor about how no-one ever considered her feelings. When the counsellor commented on the contrast between Fiona's anger towards her tutor, who had offered her both an explanation for his absence as well as an alternative appointment the very next day, and her apparent equanimity towards the counsellor who had given no reason for cancelling her session nor another to replace it, Fiona said that the two situations were completely different. Her tutor was paid to teach her, she explained, while the counsellor was trying to help her. Here we can see how Fiona has split off her feelings of disapointment and anger about her counsellor's cancellation of her session and attributed them instead to her tutor. In this way she is able to deny her feelings of disappointment in relation to the counsellor and to protect their relationship, which she has found helpful, from any angry and destructive feelings arising out of this. Not only does Fiona claim not to mind about her counsellor's cancellation of their session but she also further blackens her tutor by suggesting his interest in her is only financial, overlooking, of course, that her counsellor too is paid to see her. While this strategy of making her tutor bear the brunt of her feelings towards her counsellor enables Fiona to remain unaware of her negative feelings towards her counsellor, it has a potentially damaging effect on her relationship with her tutor.

Let us return to our example of a hungry baby. We have looked at our baby's response to the frustration of his need, in this case, to be fed and how he deals with this by the mechanism of splitting described earlier. While splitting can be effective in separating good and bad experiences, there remains the problem of how to deal with the bad feelings themselves. The process that typically accompanies splitting and enables the individual to rid himself of bad or unwanted feelings is termed *Projection*. Projection refers to the expulsion of unwanted or unacceptable thoughts or feelings from the self and their relocation elsewhere, either in another person or in an inanimate object. While splitting and projection are ubiquitous processes and can provide temporary relief in emotionally painful situations, their excessive or persistent use is generally harmful.

This is demonstrated in the example above in which Fiona makes use of splitting and projection to deal with potentially difficult feelings about her counsellor by splitting them off and projecting them onto her tutor so that he is now experienced as the cause of her feelings of anger and disappointment. Thus, while Fiona succeeded in making her tutor the villain of the piece, and in keeping her counsellor free of blame, she was still left with intense angry feelings towards her tutor which, if she acted upon them, might damage her relationship with her tutor and have disastrous consequences for her studies. In this case Fiona needs to be able to refrain from acting upon feelings of hurt and anger which, at a conscious level, are felt in relation to her tutor and, at an unconscious level, are determined by her counsellor's cancelling her session. If she is able to hold on to her feelings for long enough, it may be possible for her counsellor to help her understand that her anger towards her tutor is misdirected and that it would be self-destructive to miss the alternative appointment offered by him. The complementary process to projection is *Internalisation*. Internalisation describes the taking into the self of some aspect of a relationship and, together with projection, is central to the individual's development of the capacity to tolerate and understand his feelings.

The ability to tolerate feelings, especially of a destructive nature, without impulsively resorting to action is gradually developed over time. In order to understand how this capacity for containing one's feelings evolves, we have to return to the primary relationship between mother and baby in which the mother acts as the container for feelings that the baby cannot yet manage. To illustrate this process we can look at what happens, for example, when an infant is crying and his mother is not initially present. We might surmise that the baby is being assailed by painful feelings that he cannot relieve himself of and that, unable to help himself, he is signalling his distress through his cries. In the normal course of events, his mother will hear his cries and come to see what is wrong – perhaps he has become aware of his mother's absence and feels frightened. He may stop crying as soon as he sees her or she may need to pick him up and comfort him, in either case his mother's response and proximity is sufficient to relieve him of his distress on this occasion. Here we might say that his mother has been able to respond to her baby's anxiety in such a way as to enable him to regain his sense of well-being. Under these favourable circumstances the baby has undergone an unpleasant experience *but*, and this is the crucial point, the level of anxiety he has experienced did not exceed his capacity to bear it because of his mother's timely intervention. He has therefore had an experience of anxiety that can be endured, or to put it another way, it was not the end of the world after all when his mother disappeared for a short while. Not only does his mother need to be able to gauge how much anxiety he can tolerate, in other words, how long can she leave him before stepping in to help out, but also she has to determine how much anxiety *she* can bear before having to intervene.

Individuals vary enormously in their capacity to bear anxiety and the ability to judge this is an extremely important part of the counsellor's task. The following example illustrates the type of difficulty that may be encountered in making such an assessment. Betty, a final year medical student, telephoned her counsellor two days after her weekly session which was on a Tuesday. She had recently had an HIV test following an accident with a syringe in casualty and while there was very little risk that she had contracted the HIV virus, she had been advised to have the test as a matter of routine. She had been feeling extremely anxious about the result and wanted to know if the counsellor could see her again that week. Betty was a calm and thoughtful student and the counsellor was surprised and concerned by the urgency of her request. Since there were no sessions available for the rest of the week the counsellor offered to see Betty for fifteen minutes at the end of the next day which Betty gratefully accepted. In weighing up the situation the counsellor had in mind that Betty's elder brother had died in a car accident when she was ten years old and that Betty had felt guilty that she had survived the accident. The counsellor had been struck by the intensity of Betty's anxiety about the HIV test and she had wondered if Betty's potentially fatal accident with the syringe had stirred up overwhelming feelings she had experienced in relation to the fatal car accident many years ago. On the basis that Betty may have been re-experiencing a level of anxiety that was beyond her capacity to bear, the counsellor had offered to see her before her next due session. When she saw her the next day, Betty was much calmer and she told the counsellor that knowing she had been able to come and talk about her feelings today had helped a great deal. Betty confirmed thinking about her brother and she recalled that after her brother's death her parents had both been too distraught to consider her feelings and that when they were more available she had not wanted to upset them again by talking about how she felt. In this example we can see that the counsellor has judged that the anxiety Betty was currently experiencing was greater than she could reasonably tolerate and that she needed the counsellor to help her manage it. We might ask what would have happened if the counsellor had been unable or unwilling to meet Betty's demand for additional help. One possibility is that Betty would have reacted as she did with her parents after her brother's death, that is, by suppressing her feelings and once again losing the opportunity for receiving help in managing her feelings.

The process of *Containment* described above is not a passive one, rather it involves the mother and her infant in an active and interactive process in which the baby passes his unbearable feelings to his mother who, provided she is not overwhelmed by them herself, receives and translates his feelings into a tolerable experience which she then passes back to him. This process is easily recognisable in the common scenario of a child who, having fallen and scraped his knee, runs tearfully to his mother who 'kisses it better'. In the course of this exchange the child experiences relief from being helped by his mother with his immediate pain. However, he also makes a significant developmental gain through this interaction with his mother in that he takes something of her containing function into himself so that the next time he hurts himself, he will have acquired some capacity to manage his pain by himself. Gradually, over the course of time, the child will become able to pick himself up after a fall without having to go to his mother for help. Of course, a mother who finds it difficult to manage her own anxieties about her child may panic when he comes to her with some injury or other. In this case she will be less able to help her child in developing an ability to manage painful feelings and sensations. While the capacity to contain and tolerate feelings is clearly of enormous importance, a further process is required in order to manage feelings effectively, and this involves making sense of them. Thus, a mother may be able to soothe her baby's cries for food by picking him up, however at some point, unless she understands what his crying is about and attends to it, he will start crying again. At this stage, the baby needs his mother to make sense of his feelings for him and, in the ordinary course of events, this is what she does. In other words, she thinks about the meaning of his feeling state for him and then converts this into some appropriate action, in this instance feeding him. Not only does he get fed but he also takes in the experience of being understood and this, along with countless more similar experiences, forms the basis for the development of his own capacity to make sense of his feelings. It is of course inevitable that on many occasions his mother will not be able to tune in immediately to his emotional state and that he will therefore experience some frustration of his needs while his mother tries to work out what it is that he needs. Provided that his level of frustration remains within tolerable limits then this experience too, of having to wait, will help him to be able to tolerate minor frustrations in the future. The importance of learning both to tolerate uncomfortable feelings and to think about them is illustrated in the following example.

Matthew had been recommended to see a counsellor by his GP whom he had visited more or less weekly since starting university. Essentially Matthew was plagued by one anxiety after another about his health. The problems he reported to his GP were all of a minor nature and were infrequent in occurrence. For example, he had occasional difficulty in getting off to sleep at night, headaches that turned out to be consequential on a night in the pub, the odd bout of diarrhoea or constipation and so on. The reason Matthew gave for going to his GP with this steady stream of worries was that his symptoms might be indicative of some grave illness and it was better to be safe than sorry. His GP had initially accepted this rationale and Matthew had been grateful for her continued reassurances that there was nothing seriously wrong with him. On his last visit Matthew's GP had suggested that there might be some psychological problem underlying his health worries and referred him for counselling. Matthew had made an appointment to see a counsellor immediately and he was patently anxious when he arrived for his initial session. Why, he nervously asked, had his GP referred him, what did she think was wrong, did the counsellor think he would be all right? The counsellor remarked that he seemed to need her to reassure him, like his GP, that there was nothing wrong with him. Matthew agreed and asked again if she thought he would be all right. The counsellor suggested that perhaps they could think *together* about why he found it so difficult to work out for himself whether he was all right or not. It emerged that Matthew's mother 'lived on her nerves', as he put it. Matthew was her only child and his father had left not long after his birth. His mother had always worried about his health and at the slightest sign of ill health would take him off to see the doctor whom he recalled as a kind and grandfatherly sort of a man. Thus it would seem that in the absence of a husband with whom she could share her anxieties about her son, Matthew's mother took them to her doctor, a man who was endlessly willing to reassure her. Here we can see that Matthew's mother had never been able to contain her anxiety about his health and now, neither could he. In this context, it is worth noting that the counsellor did not concede to Matthew's need for reassurance directly, instead she offered to think about it with him. In taking this step, she was conveying to Matthew the idea that his anxieties could be withstood and, hopefully, eventually be understood.

In the discussion above we have begun to describe how the individual develops the capacity to contain and make sense of his emotional experiences through his relationships, initially with his mother and later with others. Two of the most important mechanisms that underlie the processes by which these capabilities are established, projection and internalisation, have also been described. Returning to the mother and her infant, we can describe the process of containment using the mechanisms of projection and internalisation thus: the infant projects his bad feelings, for example, the emotional distress aroused by hunger, into his mother who accepts them and makes sense of them. She recognises that he is hungry and feeds him and he then internalises the positive experience of having a mother who can understand and satisfy him. This, along with further experiences of having his feelings understood and met, will form the embryo of his capacity for self-knowledge.

The provision of a containing relationship within which the development of self-understanding is encouraged, is one of the primary tasks of psychodynamic counselling. In the example above, it is clear that Matthew was not able to manage his feelings of anxiety about his health on his own and constantly sought reassurance from parental figures. He projected his feelings into his mother, the family doctor and more recently, the college doctor and in this way received temporary relief from his anxieties. There are two points about the persistence of Matthew's health worries that are relevant to our discussion here. The first is that no one seemed able to provide him with any lasting relief from his anxieties and the second is that he was unable to reassure himself. With regard to these points we could say that Matthew had failed to internalise an experience of a relationship in which his anxiety could be adequately contained and understood and that that is why he could not reassure himself. Instead of internalising a satisfactory containing function Matthew had taken in an experience from his relationship with his mother in which anxiety could not be managed by the self. In simple terms, he had learned that the way to deal with his anxieties about himself was to go to the doctor. While this strategy appeared to have worked while Matthew was still living at home and attending his family doctor, it was less effective when he started university. The doctor at the university's health centre recognised that Matthew's concerns about his health did not justify his high level of attendance at the surgery. In recommending that Matthew go for counselling, the doctor was conveying her belief that Matthew's fears about his health could not be satisfactorily understood, and therefore treated, within a medical framework. While the doctor's recognition that there might be something else wrong with him increased Matthew's level of anxiety, it also served to move him into a setting in which he might finally begin to address the underlying reasons for his anxiety. Matthew began his counselling session by trying to make the counsellor into a figure who, like his family doctor, would accept his projections and reassure him. While the counsellor acknowledged his wish for reassurance she did not comply with it and instead proposed that they might try to understand his desire to be comforted rather than act upon it. In this way the counsellor had provided Matthew with an elementary experience of being with someone who believed that anxiety could be contained and understood. Obviously one such event is unlikely to make much impact upon a lifetime's experiences to the contrary and many such exposures would be needed to encourage the development of a self-containing function.

It is not surprising that the nature of the infant's relationship with his mother plays such a vital part in his psychological development. It is the first, and therefore prototypical, relationship that the individual has, and it is inevitable that it will influence subsequent relationships. From the discussion above it follows that the child whose mother is affectively attuned to him will internalise an experience of being adequately understood and will therefore grow into an adult who can tolerate and make sense of his feelings. However, there are many factors which can interfere with this course of development. For example, babies vary enormously from the moment of birth in their capacity to bear frustration and a mother's ability to comfort her baby will be considerably determined by his apparent level of need. Generally speaking, the easier it is for a mother to meet her baby's demands, the more gratifying it is for her and a mutually satisfying relationship ensues. Where problems arise, for example, when a mother has difficulty in feeding her baby, anxiety and frustration come to dominate the interaction between mother and child and dissatisfaction results. Of course, a mother's ability to manage her baby will depend both on her own experiences of being cared for herself which *she* has internalised *and* on the level of support and understanding she has available to her. For example, in the case described above, Matthew's father was not at hand to help his mother manage her anxieties about him.

While the child's relationship with his mother is crucial, other family relationships play a formative part in the individual's development and we will look next at the role of the father.

The role of the father

When the baby is very young, the father's principal role tends to be one of providing protection and support for the baby's mother in order that she can be free to divert her energies towards looking after their child. The very close relationship that is built up between mother and baby inevitably excludes the father to some extent and may be experienced by some fathers as painful. However, for others their role as both protector of, and provider for, this relationship between mother and baby is deeply satisfying and mitigates against potential feelings of jealousy. Whatever the father's reaction to this special relationship from which he is to some extent excluded, he has a critical role to play in eventually interrupting it. The reasons underlying the importance of the father's intrusion into the mother–child relationship are various and inter-related. First and foremost, however, is the challenge it poses to the infant's fantasies about himself and his world. Whereas, previously, he had every reason to believe that his mother loved only him and was totally his to command, he now has to contend with the realisation that he is not the only object of love in his mother's eyes. While this blow to his self-esteem is a painful one, there is a potential compensation to soften it, namely the acquisition of a father. However, in order to be able to move on and develop his relationship with his father, he has first to relinquish his exclusive relationship with his mother. This process, whereby something has to be given up to enable progress to a subsequent stage of development, involves loss and is therefore intrinsically painful. The conflict between staying with what is safe and known and venturing into new and unfamiliar territory continues throughout life and is often apparent in the difficulties some students experience when they leave home to study further afield. We will explore this issue in more depth in Chapter 3.

The baby's loss of his exclusive rights to his mother is compensated partly by the procurement of a father and also by the experience of being looked after by a couple. Although the child has now to share his parents, there are considerable advantages to him in this new arrangement of a threesome. For example, the knowledge that the parents have each other for support means that he need not feel solely responsible for either of them and this gives him a great deal more freedom in his own life. However, as the following example shows, such shifts in existing family relationships may not always be perceived in such a positive light. Christopher sought the help of a counsellor at his college because his father had recently been made redundant and he was very worried about how his mother would cope with having his father 'under her feet all the time'. Christopher was in his final year and he was finding it very hard to concentrate on his work because of his concerns about his mother. His father had held a prestigious position in publishing and Christopher felt that he had always put his work before family life. He had been a largely absent father and Christopher recalled many family holidays without his father who was unable to accompany them because of work commitments. His mother was a shy retiring woman and, aside from some voluntary work for the local church, she had few social contacts. However, she was a keen water-colour painter and had sold some of her work, principally through business acquaintances of his father. While his mother had always been sympathetic to his and his brother's complaints about their father's absences and also missed her husband, she nevertheless remained supportive of him. When the counsellor asked Christopher what he was afraid would happen if his father was at home with his mother all day, he realised that he did not really know why he felt uneasy about the situation. It then emerged that his father had in fact taken voluntary redundancy and that he and Christopher's mother had planned a long holiday abroad together after which they intended to set up in business on their own. Following exploration of Christopher's long-held grievance against his father for not being more available to him, his current concern about how his parents would get along together was eventually understood in terms of *his* feelings of jealousy and of being excluded from a closer relationship with his father. Thus, rather than face up to painful feelings about the new level of intimacy between his mother and father, he turned the situation around into one that he could tolerate, where his mother and father would not get on. Although this created problems for him in as much as he was now worried about his mother, it was the less painful situation because it allowed him to maintain the fiction of being more important to his mother than was his father. In order to free himself of his anxieties about his mother and get on with his college work he needed to be able to acknowledge that his mother had his father and did not need him. Christopher had found it more difficult than usual to give up his fantasy of an exclusive relationship with his mother because he had not had the opportunity for establishing a satisfying relationship with his father when younger.

There are, of course, many potential impediments to the transition from the absorption and exclusivity of a two-person relationship to relationships in which concern for the needs of others and the capacity for sharing become important. Some mothers find it difficult to give up the special relationship they develop with their child and feel jealous of anyone who threatens their sense of primacy. Such feelings may not be conscious but nevertheless may be subtly communicated to the child and can have potentially damaging consequences for both parties. The following example illustrates one such case. Marta, an only child, had always enjoyed a close relationship with her mother whom she regarded more as a friend. The two often went out together and her father, a businessman whose work regularly took him abroad, was grateful that his wife and daughter got on so well since he felt guilty about his frequent trips. Neither parent put any overt pressure on Marta to stay at home, however, when she chose to attend a university in her home town and to continue living at home, her father was relieved. Marta's first year at university went well and she and three other girls on her course became close friends. Marta's mother liked her daughter's new friends and encouraged her to bring them home and she often cooked for them. Everything seemed fine until Marta told her mother that she and her friends had decided to share a flat during their second year. Her mother felt hurt and perplexed by Marta's wish to leave home. She asked Marta what was wrong with living at home and when Marta said that there was nothing wrong but that she wanted to live with her friends, her mother began to cry and pleaded with her to stay. The following few weeks at home were tense. Her mother refused to discuss the matter and was generally cold towards Marta. It was at this point that Marta sought help from a counsellor. She felt angry and frustrated with her mother but also guilty for hurting her and she could not foresee any solution to their situation. The counsellor was struck that Marta did not mention her father once and therefore asked Marta about her father's view. It transpired that Marta had not told her father about her desire to leave home, however she remarked that he often told her stories about the fun he had had sharing a flat when he was a student. Marta then asked the counsellor directly whether she thought she was selfish for wanting to live with her friends. Recognising this as an appeal to a third party who might be able to act as an intermediary between Marta and her mother, the counsellor observed that Marta had perhaps overlooked her father as a potential source of help. Marta thought that her father would be annoyed at being asked to intercede between them and that, in any event, he would side with her mother. However, she accepted that she did not actually *know* how he would react. After a further few sessions in which Marta's role in compensating her mother for her father's absences was explored, Marta finally spoke to her father about her predicament. To her surprise, he was sympathetic and sorry that she had not spoken to him sooner. He reminded her of how much he had enjoyed living with his friends as a student and assured her that he would talk with her mother. Despite her mother's continued opposition, Marta went ahead with her plans and moved in with her friends. Relations between her parents became increasingly acrimonious and eventually reached crisis point when Marta elected to spend her birthday with her friends rather than with her family. Following advice from a family friend, her parents went for marital therapy. Some months later Marta reported that the situation at home had improved considerably and that while her mother still missed her badly, she no longer tried to make Marta feel guilty for leaving. In this example, we can see how Marta's over-involved relationship with her mother was disguising difficulties in her parent's marriage and that when the mask was removed these became apparent. In seeking the help of someone outside her relationship with her mother, Marta was indicating her need for a third party to come between them. In this case the counsellor responded by helping Marta to mobilise her father's assistance.

At another level, this example also illustrates the importance of the father's role in introducing reality into the life of the child. Put simply, the father's intervention shatters the child's fantasy that the world consists of only he and his mother. On the one hand this is a relief because it means that there is someone other than himself to look after his mother, but on the other hand it is a profound disillusionment. Not only is he not his mother's only love, he is not even her first love! However, as discussed above, there is the compensation of gaining a father.

In the previous section concerning the relationship between mother and child, the importance of internalising a maternal containing function was discussed. Of course this is only one of many aspects of his relationship with his mother that the child internalises and, in a similar vein, the child also internalises facets of his relationship with his father. These internalised characteristics form the basis for the common observation that children are, in character, often very much like their mothers and fathers. It also accounts for the fact, often indiscernible to the individual, that he will be inclined to relate to others in a fashion that bears considerable similarity to his parents' modes of relating. This tendency to behave as one's parents often goes unrecognised and when pointed out to the individual may come as a surprise as the following example illustrates. Sunil was having problems with his flatmates whom he portrayed as selfish and inconsiderate. He complained that he could not study because they played music loudly and watched television till late, that they took his food without asking, that they didn't wash or clear up after them, and so on. He felt that he had little choice but to find somewhere else to live. When asked how his flatmates had responded to his complaints, Sunil said that he had not actually spoken to them about his concerns. Sunil's reluctance to confront his flatmates stemmed from an anxiety that he would lose control and over-react and that his flatmates would laugh at him. Subsequent exploration of his family background revealed that Sunil's father was a somewhat embittered man whose business endeavours had failed to reach his expectations. He complained endlessly to the family about the shortcomings of his workers, however, he never voiced his dissatisfactions to them directly, claiming that they would only ignore him. Sunil felt that his father should say something to his staff. He could not understand his father's unwillingness to act and considered his inaction 'pathetic'. When the parallel with his own situation was drawn to his attention, Sunil was taken aback. He could, however, recognise that there were similarities and that both he and his father drew back from challenging others for fear of being ridiculed. In this case we can see how Sunil had taken into himself his father's fear that his feelings would not be treated with respect with the result that he was afraid to express and use his feelings effectively.

The continuing process of identification with one's parents through internalisation of aspects of one's parents is largely unconscious and this probably accounts for the blindspots people may have to the similarities between themselves and their parents. While these may be blindingly obvious to family and friends, the individual may fail to recognise the parental connection. For example, an individual who has a poor relationship with a parent may feel disinclined to recognising any links with them. This was the case with Sandra who described her mother disparagingly as a nag. Sandra had been relieved to leave home and now shared a flat with her boyfriend. She had sought counselling because of problems with her boyfriend who she felt was behaving unreasonably. Basically, she felt that he was not doing his fair share of the household tasks and that he complained when she reminded him about things he had still to do. A typical comment from her was, 'But if I don't tell him, he'd never do anything!' Thus, Sandra had left home to escape a nagging mother only to discover that she had brought her along in herself.

Brothers and sisters

Although the average number of children per family has decreased over recent years most children still have one or more siblings. If one takes into account factors other than the number of children, such as the child's position in the family, the sex of his siblings and the age differences between siblings, it is clear that the range of potential experience among siblings is vast. A child who has no brothers and sisters will obviously have a very different childhood from a child who has several siblings. It is impossible to discuss every potential variation of the family group, especially if one also includes, adopted children, half-brothers and half-sisters and step-families. However, a feature that is common to all these different family scenarios is the necessity for accommodation and adaptation in relation to the needs and wishes of other family members. Sharing and tolerance become vital as family resources inevitably become squeezed by the demands of each new member of the family. At the same time, the capacity to compete and fight for one's share takes on a new importance and can foster the development of a competitive spirit which may find useful expression at school or later in work. Needless to say, the ruthless pursuit of one's own interests needs to be tempered with an adequate measure of concern for the interests of others and this balance is not at all easy to achieve. The following examples, which focus on relative position within the family, illustrate some of the developmental issues, and some of the problems, that can arise in relation to one's siblings. The first example looks at an aspect of the position of the so called 'middle child', the second addresses a problem arising out of being the youngest child while the third example explores some of the difficulties attendant on being the eldest. It should perhaps be emphasised that order of birth does not on its own lead to specific types of problems. The examples that follow have been chosen to illustrate how birth order can *interact* with other factors to produce particular difficulties in the development of the individual.

Selina was the middle of three girls, her elder sister was two years older and her younger sister was three years her junior. She came with no central identifiable problem but generally felt miserable and discontent. Though she lacked enthusiasm for her studies, her course work was not a cause for concern to her. She had a reasonable social life and was in a stable relationship with her boyfriend of whom she was fond. Her parents lived within easy reach and she visited home every weekend though, on reflection, she thought that she didn't enjoy her visits that much. Her elder sister had never left home and had attended a local college before finding employment in the small town in which they lived. Her younger sister, who was living at home, attended a local sixth-form college where she was working towards her A-levels. Selina felt that her parents didn't show much interest in her life and she complained that they always talked to her about her sisters when she came home. Her elder sister had always been close to their mother and Selina felt jealous of their relationship. Her younger sister was a tomboy and shared her father's enthusiasms for sport and cars and had an easy jocular relationship with him. Selina felt that she didn't have a special relationship with anyone and she carried her resentment about this into the rest of her life where it was echoed in her lacklustre attitude to people and activities. Thus she could not take a special interest in her course nor, for example, could she allow herself to feel special in her relationship with her boyfriend because that would mean giving up the resentment, initially held towards her parents, that she now bore towards the world as a whole. In this example we can see that Selina reacted against her sense of exclusion from an intimate relationship with either of her parents by angrily turning away from them, thereby further distancing herself. After a turbulent adolescence, she had left home at the earliest opportunity, only to return each weekend and have her grievances reinforced.

Ian was the youngest of four children by six years and had twin brothers and a sister. In some ways he had felt like an only child because by the time he was six years old all his siblings had left home, his sister had gone to boarding school and his brothers to university. He had always been 'the baby' in the family and his precocity could be understood both as a counter to this role as well as a collusion with it. He was a serious-minded teenager and had eschewed the company of other children in favour of spending his time with his parents and their friends who found him amusing. The problem he had now at university was that he was unable to establish friendships with his fellow students. He was simultaneously afraid of and contemptuous of them. He feared he would not fit in and, because of this anxiety, he poured scorn on their interests and activities which further alienated him from them. He described how he would sit in the corner of the local student pub with a drink and a serious novel, while out of the corner of his eye he would watch the other students laughing and joking with one another. On one such occasion a student from one of his classes called over to him to join them. He longed to say yes, saunter over and join in the fun, instead he felt himself become anxious and, pointing to his book he grinned and left. It gradually became clear that Ian had hated being treated like a child. He had longed to be grown-up like his brothers and sister and had disliked intensely their, as he felt it, mockery of him for being 'a baby'. As a child, he would bite his lip rather than cry out and on the rare occasions when he could not do something for himself, he found it humiliating to ask for help. However, now that he was grown-up he could not bear the thought that others might see through his facade of self-sufficiency.

Lindsey was two years older than her brother, Jack, and three years older than her sister, Emily. She was very much aware of being the big sister and she had come for counselling because she had realised that her tendency to adopt this role was adversely affecting her friendships at college. Recently she had blown up at a friend, Clare, who had let her down over a relatively trivial issue and she had felt stung when Clare had angrily told her that she was fed up with her insufferable bossiness. She explained that she and some friends had planned a day trip to the coast. Lindsey had taken it upon herself to organise everyone and had delegated various tasks. Clare's job had been to buy disposable glasses, plates and cutlery. Clare had left things to the last minute and had been unable to find any plastic cups by the time they were due to leave. She had apologised and suggested that they could buy some when they got to the coast, but Lindsey had exploded and her anger had cast a shadow over the trip. Lindsey recognised that she had over-reacted and that they could have bought the cups later and she had no idea why she had felt so angry with Clare at the time. Exploration of her role as big sister in her family revealed that her mother had suffered from a lengthy period of depression after her own mother's death. Lindsey was around ten years old when her grandmother died. Her father was unable to cope with three young and active children as well as a depressed wife. Normally a fairly easy going man he now lost his temper at the slightest provocation and she recalled frequent rows which usually ended with her mother in tears. Terrified by her father's unreasonable angry outbursts, Lindsey quickly learned to round up her brother and sister when her father came home from work and to organise games to keep them quiet. She also recalled helping her mother out at meal times and in bathing the younger children. Her efforts did not go unnoticed and her grateful mother often said that she did not know what she would have done without her. Her brother and sister, on the other hand, resented her control over them. Lindsey was able to recognise that her terror that her father might find something out of place, lose his temper and shout at her mother, underlay her need to be in charge of things. Thus, when Clare failed to get the glasses as instructed, Lindsey felt that the situation was no longer under her control, and this frightened her. In this situation, Lindsey's unreasonable outburst of anger could be understood in terms of an identification with her father who had been unable to manage his feelings in the wake of his wife's depression.

These examples illustrate how one aspect of family life, namely position in the family, may be helpful in understanding the development of the individual. There are, of course, very many other important factors concerning the relationships between siblings that need to be borne in mind. For example, in cultures where boys are valued more highly than girls (a not uncommon feature of many Asian families), issues arising out of envy, jealousy, resentment, low self-esteem and so on may be especially relevant. Whatever the particular circumstances, each addition to the family requires an element of adjustment from the rest of the family and the relative success with which this is met can sometimes be gauged at a later stage in the individual's life, as illustrated in the following example. Brian, who came from a large Irish family, was finding it difficult to settle into halls. It was his first year at university and the first time he had lived away from home. Somewhat surprisingly, given his numerous brothers and sisters, he found the noise and bustle of life in student halls distressing. He reported that despite feeling tired it was very hard for him to get off to sleep and that when he was awake he felt restless and unable to concentrate on his work. When asked about his childhood, Brian, who was the third of eight children, recalled that his mother had been dangerously ill following the birth of her fourth child, and that he had even been afraid that his mother would die. While this immediate danger had passed relatively swiftly, his father had been preoccupied with his wife and the new baby and had had little time for Brian and his two brothers. Although an aunt had come to help out, he could not remember her being there, he could only recall his intense fears about losing his mother. It seemed as though his enormous anxiety that his mother might die had wiped out even this helpful aunt. After a week or so his mother came home with the new baby and the situation at home gradually returned to normal. Many years later, his mother told him that she had been surprised by his coolness on her return, the more so because he had previously been very attached to her. Brian was not close to his baby brother and he remained somewhat aloof from the brother and sisters that followed. It was as though they had taken his beloved mother from him, which in a particular sense was true. He *had* lost his place as his mother's 'baby' to another and it seemed that he had never really got over this trauma. Thus, his response to the arrival of his siblings had taken the form of a withdrawal from his mother and a distant relationship with his siblings. Brian's problem in settling in halls could now be understood in terms of a repetition of his original traumatic separation from his mother which had been stimulated by the move from home to university. In this light, the disturbing students represented the other children with whom he would now be forced to share his home and, of course, his mother.

Peer relationships

The establishment of peer relationships represents a further level of development for the individual and can sometimes, if necessary, helpfully mitigate against an unfavourable situation at home. While pre-school age children certainly form relationships with their peers, their primary attachment to their parents, and especially to their mother, usually pre-empt strong and lasting peer relationships. However, the gradual detachment from parents, encouraged by starting school, is generally accompanied by an increasing interest in, and attachment to, their peers. At this stage, the child's disinterest in the sex of their prospective friends begins to give way and a strong preference for same sex friendships starts to become apparent. Relationships at this age tend to be intense, albeit often short lived, and are heavily coloured by the child's primary relationships. In other words the need to be closely attached to another is the paramount factor and the actual character of the other child is less important at this stage. This is the age at which best friends may be made and lost in a day! As the child grows more independent and separate from his parents, his need to develop his own identity becomes imperative and this prompts his search for others with whom he can identify. Other children of the same sex are now preferred and children begin to form themselves into like minded groups, gangs or cliques. They gain a sense of their own identity through being part of a group and it is therefore especially painful for individuals who cannot gain access to a group. Of course, a group partly constructs its identity, and maintains its integrity, on the basis of who it excludes and the struggle to be part of the 'in' group can be a fraught one during childhood and adolescence. Children, especially younger children who have not yet developed much of a sense of concern for the needs of others, can be cruel and insensitive to children who they perceive as weaker than themselves and excluding other children from their groups can be one powerful way in which such cruelty becomes manifest. Groups, because of the particular dynamics that they foster, confer upon children a sense of power that they do not feel in possession of when they are on their own. (This accounts, in part, for the disbelief that many parents express when told of some misdemeanour their child has been involved in as part of a group.) However, because personal responsibility is effectively abnegated and projected onto the group or group leader, the individual feels free to act in ways he might otherwise abjure.

For example, Alan was a shy, rather self-effacing physics student. He had been strongly encouraged to see a counsellor following an incident in which he, along with several other students, had been given an official warning to the effect that any further offence would result in expulsion from university. On the day of the incident in question, Alan had been in a physics practical class when the fire alarm sounded. He went out into the corridor along with other students from his class and was heading down the stairs when one of them shouted out to go up to the coffee bar on the next floor. One or two girls who were ahead of him carried on down the stairs but several of his classmates, most of the boys in fact, turned round and followed the one who had shouted out. Alan had felt torn, he knew that he should continue downstairs but he wanted to join in the excited crowd of boys that was rushing upstairs. He turned round and followed the group up to the coffee bar which was now empty. Along with the other boys, he crammed his pockets full of chocolate bars. He had watched, fascinated, as two of the other boys had tried to prise the cash register open. At this point a porter who had come to check that the fire doors were shut spotted them. At the sight of this sign of authority, Alan's feelings of excitement drained away and he was left feeling sick with fear. Talking about the incident later with the counsellor, he remembered how frightened he had used to be of his father when he was young and how lonely he had felt at school because his father would not let him play after school with the other boys in his class. His father, a teacher at the school, had considered the other boys who came mainly from the local estate, a bad influence and forbade Alan from meeting them outside school. Alan never stood up to his father and was an obedient and well-behaved child. His behaviour during the fire alarm was therefore out of character, indeed he had surprised himself by his actions and was ashamed of the part he had played. The central factor in under-standing Alan's uncharacteristic behaviour was his intense fear of and consequent acquiescence to authority, as a result of which he had repressed all his rebelliousness. The fire alarm incident afforded him the opportunity to express some of this by opposing one author-ity (the university) under the protection of another authority, namely the group with whom he had raided the coffee bar. However, with the collapse of the authority of the students' group and the return of the old regime, Alan immediately began to fear reprisals from the university authorities. In this case, Alan had been temporarily able to overcome his fear of his father/the university and join the other boys in his class in a rebellious act by aligning himself with the authority of the group.

For many students, contact with their peer group reaches a peak during their university years. Not only do students spend most of their working and leisure time with their peers, but also, many live in rented accommodation with other students and holidays are often spent travelling together. The capacity to form satisfactory and supportive relationships is therefore of paramount importance. In Chapter 5 we will look more closely at some of the factors which may underlie problems in forming adequate relationships. However, in the context of this chapter on development, it should be noted that many relationships formed at this stage can be seen to reflect a reworking of earlier family relationship dynamics, and sometimes with the same frustrating outcomes. For example, Dorothy came for counselling because she was feeling depressed and because her friends had told her they were fed up with her moodiness. They urged her to get some help. She complained angrily that her friends took her for granted and that no one ever thought to do anything for her in return. The problem was that she enjoyed helping people out and doing them unexpected favours, but then felt angry and resentful when they did not do the same for her. On the other hand, when her friends did do something for her, Dorothy found it difficult to appreciate their efforts. Dorothy's mother was a busy and ambitious business woman with little time left over for the family. As a child, Dorothy had been jealous of other girls who had what she called 'proper mothers' by which she meant mothers who baked cakes, cooked Sunday dinners, helped with homework, were at home after school, and so on. As she grew older she took it upon herself to fill this gap and she did such things as cooking for the family, helping her younger sister with her homework and ironing her father's shirts. In this way, then, she became the sort of mother she had longed for and this gave her a sense of satisfaction – at the same time, however, she resented the fact that there was still no one to do the same for her, as a result of which she would become bad tempered and irritable. Clearly, Dorothy's continuing and unresolved longing for someone who might attend to her was being replayed in her relationships with her friends. However, the extent of her needs coupled with her defence of identifying with her 'ideal' mother, made it impossible for her friends to give her anything she could truly appreciate. To put it another way, Dorothy was using her relationships with her friends to create the perfect mother–daughter relationship she felt she had missed as a child. When she played the role of the perfect mother she felt happy and satisfied but when she wanted to take the other role, to play the daughter of such a perfect mother, there was no one available to play the mother of Dorothy's fantasies and this enraged her.

Of course, peer relationships also afford valuable opportunities to rework old relationship problems in new and creative ways and for many students, it can be an enormous relief to find like minds and to realise that their concerns are shared. At a time in their lives when many young people feel out of touch with their parents and their parents' generation, their peer group can provide an important point of reference and support. This breach with their parents' ideas and attitudes has less to do with the content of parental beliefs as such and can be more easily understood in terms of the child's need to develop his own ideas, in other words, it is part of the child's struggle to develop his own identity. For some students, the freedom afforded by university comes as a breath of fresh air after the constraining and perhaps stifling atmosphere of home and school. These are, in the main, students who have outgrown the family nest and are eager to try out their wings. For others, however, who are not yet ready to take control of their lives and to think for themselves, the relative lack of structure arouses more anxiety than excitement. Some subjects offer more structured timetables than others and the subject chosen by the student can sometimes be seen to reflect, among other factors, the individual's attitude towards autonomous thought. Issues related to choice of subject are potentially complex and will be explored further in Chapter 6.

Personal and sexual identity

The establishment of a stable personal identity, including a clear idea about one's sexual identity, is arguably the most important task of early adulthood. Inevitably, the success attending this stage of development will depend on the strength and integrity of the foundations upon which it is built. Factors affecting the ease with which a secure sense of personal identity is built up have been described in some detail above and include the experience of reasonable and stable family relationships; for the student, a sense of self-worth gained through achievements at school and the capacity to form friendships among one's peers are also important. All of these factors will influence the success with which the next vitally important stage of development, sexual maturity, is managed. For most individuals, the changes, bodily and emotional, that accompany the onset of sexual maturation, are disturbing. They signal unequivocally the passing of childhood and the approach of adulthood and as such, they re-awaken feelings of loss. A similar process of loss, where one state has to be relinquished in order to progress to another, was described earlier, when the mother–baby dyad is given up in order to make way for the development of relationships with others, initially with the father. Again, the ingress of reality, this time in the form of physical sexual maturation, demands a psychological shift. For the individual whose childhood has been satisfying and who is ready to move on, the sadness attending the loss of childhood is compensated for by the potential excitement of new types of relationships, including sexual relationships, and the shift towards adulthood is not too painful. Where unfulfilled childhood needs remain unmet, the individual may fail to progress towards sexually mature relationships or may carry them forward into sexual relationships in the hope of finding satisfaction there.

For example, anorexia, which may result in an arrest of physical signs of sexual maturation in girls such as menstruation and development of breasts, is often indicative of conflicts around issues of dependence and growing up. In particular, because the anorectic girl may harbour intensely ambivalent feelings towards her mother, often unconsciously, the ordinary course of progress towards sexual maturity through identification with her mother, stirs up enormous anxiety and is therefore resisted. In simple terms, the negative aspect of the anorexic's ambivalent feelings towards her mother, which are often unconscious, make it difficult for her to become like her. At the other extreme, promiscuous sexual behaviour may reflect unsatisfied longings for intimacy as a child. Marie, an attractive and ebullient young woman, came for counselling because she was fed up with her pattern of, as she put it, 'jumping into bed' with men whenever she felt low. She spoke of her behaviour in a self-mocking and admonishing tone. Enquiry about her family suggested an unsympathetic attitude in relation to weakness and need. The counsellor therefore suggested to Marie that perhaps 'jumping into bed' was her way of trying to get close to someone when she felt empty. Marie looked tearful and turned away. In recognising the longing for intimacy underlying Marie's promiscuous behaviour, the counsellor had touched upon a painful issue, namely the conflict in Marie between the part of her that, like her mother, was intolerant of emotional need and the part of her that desired closeness.

Personal identity and sexual identity are clearly intimately related and uncertainty and confusion about the latter invariably affect the former. One of the more common problems that students present in this area is a fear of homosexual feelings, often the main anxiety is about how others will react, especially parents. While avoidance of the whole issue of their sexuality provides a temporary refuge from the potential problems that may arise from recognition of their feelings, it also deprives the individual of satisfaction in a significant area of their emotional life. Relationships with others who are struggling with similar emotional battles may be productive in helping the individual understand and come to terms with their own feelings. For some students, the discovery that other people have similar feelings can be an enormous relief and paves the way towards eventual acceptance of their feelings. For others, their feelings may continue to be experienced as alien and unwanted and a source of pain and humiliation to them. John came to see a counsellor worried because he did not feel particularly sexually interested in girls. He had enjoyed his first term at university and had several friends with whom he went out at the weekend. However, most of his friends now either had girlfriends or were preoccupied with finding one and were often not available at the weekend. He thought he wouldn't mind having a girlfriend himself but, when pressed, said he would rather go out with his mates. When asked if he had ever had sexual feelings towards any of his friends, his face reddened and he replied rather angrily that he wasn't 'a poof' if that was what the counsellor was suggesting. The counsellor continued by saying that an attraction to other boys, often including sexual feelings, was common among boys and that it was an ordinary part of growing up. John responded more positively to this and, with an affected casualness, confirmed overt sexual games with other boys at school. He was adamant, however, that he had no such feelings now. John's attitude towards homosexuality was evidently negative and the idea that he might be homosexual himself was abhorrent to him. At school and during his first term at college he had been able to satisfy some of his homosexual feelings, albeit in a limited way, through his social interactions. This compromise allowed him to remain unaware of the extent of his homosexual feelings and yet to find some expression of them. Now, however, this precarious balance was faltering and he was becoming painfully aware of differences between himself and his friends. While John was able to acknowledge that he did not share his friends' apparent excitement in relation to girls, he thought that perhaps it was because he was more discerning than his friends and that he would feel like them when he met the right girl. He was resolute in his unwillingness to consider any other possibilities. Here we can see how John's intense anxiety about his homosexual feelings precluded any exploration and potential understanding and integration. In Chapter 5 we will explore these and similar issues arising out of relationships at more length.

Cultural identity

The cultural context within which an individual grows and lives inevitably shapes their developing sense of identity, lending them a 'cultural identity'. The effects of culture and ethnicity on personal development are potentially wide-ranging and our discussion here will be limited to some intrapsychic ramifications. In particular we will look at how internal conflicts may arise for students whose cultural identity may be insecurely established and who may therefore be particularly vulnerable to confusions arising out of changes in their cultural environment. Essentially, cultural identity is built up through the processes of internalisation and identification described earlier in this chapter and, certainly in the early years, the child is largely unaware of this development. The child's sense of his culture as universal and 'normal' is eventually challenged by subsequent exposure to other cultures and customs. That which is unfamiliar inevitably provokes anxiety and the extent to which this stimulates interest and curiosity as opposed to fear in the growing child will depend on a variety of factors including how secure he feels within his own identity. A number of inter-related elements affect how safely rooted within his own culture an individual feels. For example, the early milieu into which the individual is born constitutes his first 'cultural' experience and the consistency and stability of this early environment contribute to his developing a secure sense of his identity. Other factors include the nature of the individual's relationship to his parents, which will affect his positive identification with them and his commitment to, and wish to embrace, their culture. His parents' own attitude to their culture will also have a significant effect. For example, Anna had been born and brought up in Scotland. Her mother was Italian and Anna had been taught to speak Italian by her from an early age. Her mother had considered it important for her children to absorb her culture and encouraged them to speak Italian within the family. Anna recalled a time when her family had moved to a new area and she had started at a new school and had stopped speaking Italian at home. Her mother had recognised that her daughter might be struggling to fit in to her new environment and thought that not speaking Italian was part of her attempt to be the same as the other children around her. Although hurt by what she felt as her daughter's implicit rejection of her culture, her mother had understood and sympathised with Anna's conflict. Within a few months Anna had settled into her new school and she started to speak Italian with her family again. In this case, Anna's good relationship with her mother and her mother's own firm cultural identity both contributed to Anna's positive identification with her Italian origins; these two factors also enabled her mother to continue to support Anna through a period of insecurity in relation to her cultural identity.

Of course, how comfortable, or 'at home' internally, individuals feel within their culture is influenced by the degree of tolerance and understanding that their 'parent' culture enjoys within their community and among their friends. In large measure this is beyond the individual's control. However, students who feel reasonably confident in their cultural identity when leaving home for university are unlikely to feel easily threatened by unfamiliar customs and surroundings and, in most cases, will probably be able to find appropriate points of contact to support and confirm their identity. On the other hand, an environment that does not afford the individual such opportunities or that is hostile, whether overtly or covertly, to his culture, may provoke an internal crisis in the individual's relations to his cultural identity. In the following example, the absence of a suitable point of reference for important aspects of his culture led one student to reject a significant part of his identity.

Ken was in his final year when he became depressed. He was unable to concentrate on his college work and was worried about his final exams. Having done little work in the previous year, he had only just scraped through and he felt hopeless about the backlog of work he now needed to complete to pass his finals. He talked about how he had let himself and his family down. His parents, who came originally from Hong Kong, were hardworking and had little social life. His father owned three Chinese restaurants in which he and Ken's mother worked long hours and, during their free time from school, Ken and his sister helped their parents in the restaurants. At school Ken had been a diligent pupil and he had continued to work hard when he left home and started at university. In his second year he moved out of student halls and into a shared flat. His flatmates socialised most evenings and at weekends and he found it increasingly difficult to remain in the flat working while they were out enjoying themselves. Eventually he joined them. He had been alarmed by his poor academic performance at the end of the second year but had thought that he would be able to work hard and catch up in his final year. His apparent loss of his ability to apply himself in his final year seemed to underlie his sense of helplessness. A significant element of the cultural context in which Ken grew up was the high value placed upon work and, while he lived at home, this aspect of his identity was strongly reinforced within his family. The experience of living closely with students who did not share this attitude to work and who, to some extent, promoted its opposite, therefore created a severe conflict for him. His guilt about betraying his cultural identity in eschewing work for pleasure was consciously experienced by him in terms of a sense of having let his family down. At an unconscious level, the collapse of his own system of values underpinned his depressed state and contributed to his inability to work.

Many of the conflicts faced by students from minority ethnic groups when they leave their families and communities and enter university are difficult and, sometimes, impossible to resolve. The issue of arranged marriages, particularly for British students with Asian or Moslem backgrounds, is a common source of internal conflict for many young women whose cultural identity has been formed at the cusp of two very different cultures. Students whose families fear their children losing their cultural roots upon exposure to other cultures tend to be more restrictive and prohibitive, making it more difficult for these students to straddle both cultures. Rather than supporting the student in bearing the strain of accommodating to different cultures, such pressure to conform to one culture may force the student into rejecting the other leading, in extreme cases, either to the student breaking with his family or to his leaving university. Care is needed, therefore, in dealing with students faced with such conflicts, not to become drawn into taking sides and precipitating such flights but rather to provide support and to help them to think about and, where possible, to manage these conflicts. A further example of the damaging effects of conflicts related to cultural issues is described in Chapter 4 where an Indian student's 'solution' to a conflict between the expectations of his 'culture', amplified by his mother, that he would become a doctor and his own disinterest in this course led to his eventually dropping out of university.

Further reading

Hinshelwood, R. D. (1994a) *Clinical Klein,* London: Free Association Books.
Rayner, E. (1971) *Human Development,* Allen and Unwin, 3rd edn 1986.
Stern, D. (1985) *The Interpersonal World of the Infant,* New York: Basic Books.
Waddell, M. (1998) *Inside Lives: Psychoanalysis and the Growth of the Personality,* London: Duckworth.
Winnicott, D. W. (1972) *The Maturational Process and the Facilitating Environment,* London: Hogarth Press.

3

THE PRICE OF INDEPENDENCE: SEPARATION AND LOSS

In contrast to those young people who do not go on to further education after school, many students enjoy a protracted period of a number of years during which they are neither truly dependent nor independent with respect to their families. These students are in a transitional state in which they continue to draw support – material and emotional – from their families in order to prepare themselves for adulthood and an eventual break from home. This, possibly final, separation from home and family is distinguished from previous developmental stages in that there is a distinct shift in the burden of responsibility from parent to child and the ease with which this is managed is determined, to a considerable extent, by individual history. In this chapter we will be exploring some of the psychological processes involved and the factors that may affect how well separation is negotiated, such as experience of early separations during childhood. Homesickness is a common problem for new students and we will examine the different responses of two students to the experience of homesickness. Of course, when a family member leaves, for whatever reason, the entire family system is affected and the repercussions of this inevitably influence the relative success of the venture for the individual and his family; we will discuss these issues further in Chapter 4. A further important factor concerns the dependence of many students upon the state for financial support and we will return briefly to the implications of this for the development of the individual at the end of this chapter. First, however, we will consider the psychological processes underlying the student's transition from school and home to university or college.

Separation and loss

The main developmental tasks through adolescence and early adulthood involve separation from the family *and* the search for a personal identity. At the level of psychological development, this entails the evolution of a capacity to think for oneself, essentially the development of an independent mind. This developmental imperative drives the adolescent away from dependence on the ideas and ideals of his parents and their generation and towards the creation and adoption of new ideas arising out of his own peer group, giving rise to the familiar phenomenon of 'the generation gap'. This period of transition is often characterised by a violent struggle, both within the individual himself and between the individual and his parents. It is as though the ideas of the previous generation are experienced as a threat and have to be destroyed in order to make way for new growth. It is certainly the case that some parents do actively block their children's efforts to develop their own ideas – perhaps because they feel their authority to be undermined and threatened – and under these conditions an overt battle between parents and child comes as no surprise. Less expected, however, is the conflict that arises when parents do not stand in the way and instead strive to foster a tolerant environment at home. Under these circumstances, the essential *internal* nature of the struggle for independence becomes more readily apparent, where the fight is between that part of the individual that is drawn back to the comfort, familiarity and security of childhood and that other part of the self, new and strange, which yearns for the unfamiliar and the unknown. Of course, in a number of significant ways, the majority of students have already made the transition from childhood to adulthood by the time they enter university and there is, in a very real sense, 'no going back'. They have finished with school, many have left home, and most will have attained sexual maturity, at least in a physical sense, some years earlier. However, for many students, these externally visible indices of their progress towards adulthood are not accompanied by a corresponding sense of *feeling* grown-up, and the struggle towards emotional independence and maturity may continue throughout university and perhaps beyond.

In many ways, the higher education system affords the young adult an extended period during which to continue the process of separating and becoming independent. University offers a halfway house between the paternalistic protection and control of school, and the personal liability of the workplace. There is considerably less structure than at school; work and attendance are monitored less closely and the emphasis is shifted towards self-regulation and self-assessment. However, as with home and school, the relationship between the university and the individual retains parental qualities and the continuing growth and development of the individual are more or less protected and encouraged. The extension of this relationship dynamic inevitably carries with it a continuation, however attenuated, of the individual's struggle to break free from the strictures binding him to his parents. For some students the pre-eminence of their bid for independence severely interferes with their capacity to work and learn, and their time at university may become a battlefield. For these individuals, parental authority is now represented by the university and the struggle to maintain some sort of personal integrity overshadows and limits potential expansion and elaboration of the self. Because of the general tendency of adolescents to externalise the source of their inner discomfort – familiar to many parents in the accusation, 'Its all your fault!' – it can be difficult sometimes to discern the extent to which this rebellion is propelled principally by external factors, deriving from continuing parental attempts to control, and how much is internally determined and arises out of the individual's inner conflicts.

Separation inevitably involves giving up a previous state and as such always stirs up feelings of loss that have to be psychically processed. For example, a child's first day at school signifies the beginning of a new stage of his life, entailing greater separation from his mother; at the same time, it signals the end of the particular relationship that he has had with her up until then. Thus, along with the excitement that accompanies this new development in his life, the child also has to deal with the loss of his past relationship with his mother. Tearful partings and last minute embraces at the school gates are the outward evidence of an internal struggle that the child, and his mother, have to work through in order to achieve a satisfactory separation.

At the heart of the internal struggle for independence which characterises the transition from childhood into adulthood lies the matter of loss and, when they can be acknowledged, the painful feelings of depression that accompany this process. Loss is a hard and inescapable fact of life and progress. When the depressive feelings following loss can be tolerated and understood, the individual is strengthened and moves on in his life; where the pain cannot be faced and the psychic reality of the loss remains unacknowledged, then genuine progress is restricted. The former process is familiar to most people as mourning and accompanies many of the important developmental stages of life. Essentially, mourning encompasses the psychological processes that follow the loss of a loved object and that lead to the eventual relinquishing of the object. The three phases that characterise mourning are firstly denial and protest, where the idea that the loss has occurred is rejected and the individual may experience anger on account of his loss. The second stage of mourning involves resignation and acceptance of the loss, and feelings of sorrow prevail. The psychic work of the third stage is directed towards detaching from the object and, gradually, adapting to life without it. Under ordinary circumstances, the process of mourning enables the individual to recover from their loss and, in time, to feel able to form new attachments.

While grief following a death is expected, the depression that *precedes* progress is often bewildering to the individual and their close associates, often because the ambivalent feelings evoked are overlooked. For example, the feelings of sadness and, sometimes, depression that may beset new and hopeful mothers soon after the birth of their baby can be understood in some part as a response to the losses that accompany the arrival of their new baby: loss of their pregnant state; loss of their independence; and, with the advent of the 'real thing', the loss of their ideal fantasised baby. Nevertheless it still shocks the new mother and those around her that such a happy event can also carry with it such emotional pain. Similarly, it can be alarming and distressing for the new student who comes to university full of hope and expectation, to discover that instead of feeling elated he feels depressed. And yet it is a common experience among students, including those who remain living at home while they attend university. For the majority of students, as with most new mothers, this experience of depression is transitory and where there is tolerance and a sympathetic attitude in those around them, the outcome is usually favourable.

Issues of separation and loss are key to understanding one of the more common problems faced by students, namely homesickness. However, before continuing this discussion, it might be helpful at this point to consider some of the psychological mechanisms that are used to deal with feelings of loss.

Paranoid–schizoid and depressive positions; defences

In order to understand why some individuals are able to tolerate ambivalent feelings and to negotiate the various losses that accompany development more successfully than others, it is necessary to examine the underlying psychological processes involved in dealing with loss. Experientially, loss or the threat of loss leads to anxiety and the way in which the individual manages this anxiety through the course of his life can be construed developmentally, such that the capacity to bear the experience of loss, without feeling overwhelmed by it, increases with psychological maturity. One useful conceptualisation of this process involves the dynamic psychological states termed the *Paranoid–schizoid position* and the *Depressive position*. Each 'position' or state is characterised by the nature of the defence mechanisms deployed to deal with anxiety. In terms of psychological maturity, the paranoid–schizoid position is the more primitive of the two states. Essentially, both positions are an attempt to master psychic pain and distress which are aroused when the individual becomes aware of conflicting feelings or, in other words, when the individual recognises the essential ambivalence inherent in all relationships. In the paranoid–schizoid position this is primarily achieved through various mechanisms which seek to deny this emotional duality. Principal among these defences are splitting and projection (see Chapter 2), projective identification, idealisation and denigration. *Idealisation* and *Denigration* both protect the individual from becoming aware of ambivalence by over-exaggerating certain attributes and overlooking others so that, for example, the other is seen as wholly good or 'ideal' or else as wholly bad and 'denigrated'. They often occur together, though *not* contemporaneously, and are especially prevalent during adolescence. For instance, the intense idealisation of girlfriends or boyfriends that is so evident at this age is often followed by a remarkable *tour de face* when the relationship comes to an end and those previously exalted features of the beloved are now regarded with derision.

Projective identification is a more complex mechanism. It involves getting rid of unwanted or unacceptable parts of the self by projecting them into another person or thing where they can, in fantasy, be controlled or else be experienced as controlling and dangerous to the self as, for instance, in paranoid fantasies. The following example, in which unacceptable feelings of jealousy were managed by making use of projective identification, illustrates this process.

Colin, a mature student at the start of his final year, described being upset by the recent behaviour of two of his close friends from the previous year. His two friends, both on the same course as himself, had spent the summer inter-railing in Europe and though he had dearly wished to join them, his commitments at home to his partner and their new baby had ruled this out. He had been looking forward to meeting up with them again after the summer but since their return to university he had felt a distinct coolness in their manner towards him. For instance, last year they had got into the habit of going out for a drink together on Thursday nights and he had been happily anticipating continuing these evenings together. However, when he said that he was really looking forward to their next Thursday night out, his friends both said that they had too much work to do this term to spend whole evenings in the pub but that he was welcome to come over to their flat later in the evening for a drink if he wished. It was clear that Colin felt that his friends were fobbing him off with excuses about work and that they were doing so because they wanted to exclude him from their friendship. When asked why he thought that they might wish to do this, he said that last year he had gained a distinction for his dissertation and had been personally congratulated by the professor whereas one of his two friends had been lucky to scrape a pass mark for his dissertation. He thought that this friend had been jealous of his achievements and had most likely turned their other friend against him while the two of them were on holiday together in the summer. In response to an enquiry about how he had felt about his friends' summer holiday together, he said that although he would have liked the chance to travel around Europe with them, he could go round Europe another year. Half laughing, he added that his partner had been so caught up with looking after their new baby that he thought that she would probably not have noticed if he had gone anyway.

In this example there are at least two possible sources of jealousy for Colin: his friends' relationship from which he felt excluded over the summer; and his partner's relationship with their new baby. However, Colin was unaware of any feelings of jealousy in himself in relation to his friends or his partner and their baby, rather these potentially painful feelings were projected into one of his friends with whom, in Colin's mind, they were now identified. Thus Colin had rid himself of unpleasant feelings of jealousy by lodging them firmly in someone else.

Although it is often unacceptable parts of the self that are got rid of through projective identification, sometimes valued parts of the self may be projected in order to protect them from attack from other hostile elements within the self. The following, more complex, example illustrates how even positive attributes may be projected in this way.

A severely insecure young woman sought help from her university counsellor in exposing a fellow student whom she believed was stealing her ideas. While she had little concrete evidence to support her accusation of plagiarism, her conviction was unshakeable. Although a talented student, she constantly feared failure and, despite considerable academic success attesting to her abilities, she nonetheless expected that all her classmates would surpass her. In this instance, her belief that her creativity was being stolen from her was clearly paranoid and related, in part, to her intense anxiety about her capacity to keep her own creativity safe and secure from her own destructiveness. Thus, her valued creativity was projected into a fellow student – perhaps for safe keeping – and the intense anxiety aroused in relation to this loss was then experienced in terms of having been robbed. In terms of projective identification, we could say that this insecure student had projected a part of herself, namely her creativity, into another individual who, in fantasy, became identified with the projected part of herself. In this example, the student is unable to deal with the internal conflict she has between her constructive and destructive impulses. Fearful that she cannot protect the former from the latter, she splits and projects the creative part of herself only to end up feeling that something has been stolen from her. Had she projected the destructive part of herself, as she had done on numerous other occasions, then she would have ended up feeling afraid that her work would be attacked and criticised from all those individuals now identified with her hostile projections. (This is, of course, a simplification of the situation and more often than not a complex mix of both positive and negative feelings were projected at any one time.)

In the example of projective identification described above, there is a clear paranoid process in operation. However, projective identification may be used in more subtle ways, for instance, to make an unconscious communication, as illustrated in the following example. Joseph had been talking animatedly to his counsellor for about thirty minutes about various events that he felt were contributing to his feeling stressed and unable to concentrate on his university work. His counsellor was aware that she was struggling to maintain an interest in what Joseph was telling her and that she was beginning to feel irritated with him. Once or twice she interrupted his flow to make an observation about something he had said. When she had finished Joseph continued talking where he had left off, as if she had not spoken. After a while, Joseph nervously remarked that his friends sometimes got fed up with him because he talked so much. He added, with a rueful laugh, 'My mum could talk the hind legs off a donkey.' In this case we can see that by means of projective identification, Joseph has recreated an aspect of his internalised relationship with his mother in his session with the counsellor. The counsellor has been made the recipient of his projected anger towards a mother who is experienced as overwhelming and disinterested in him and whose role he enacts in relation to the counsellor. The counsellor therefore, by 'accepting' Joseph's projections, experiences countertransference feelings of helpless fury which can be used to deepen her understanding of Joseph's inner world. It is as though the only way that Joseph can effectively communicate about an aspect of his internal world is to make his counsellor experience something of it, as if to say, 'now you know what I used to feel like when my mother went on and on and didn't listen to a word I said'.

As described above, projective identification, along with other defences associated with the paranoid–schizoid position, operates principally by pre-empting any awareness of internal conflict. By contrast, defences associated with the depressive position, when ambivalent feelings can be better tolerated, function to minimise the effects of potential conflicts. These defences include repression, denial, reaction formation, undoing, isolation, internalisation, rationalisation and intellectualisation and are described below. There are many variations of these defence mechanisms, however, these will serve to illustrate how our conscious understanding may be influenced and distorted by internal mechanisms of which we are mostly unaware.

Repression, which underlies many of the other defences, is a basic and widely used mechanism of defence and operates by rendering unconscious material which might otherwise provoke conflict. *Denial* is a similar defence but differs from repression in that whereas in repression both the idea and the feeling attached to it are excluded from conscious awareness, in denial the feeling and the idea are separated and only the feeling component is repressed as illustrated in the following example. Manuel, a second year mathematics student, was advised to seek counselling on the advice of his tutor whom he had been to see following an unexpectedly poor examination result. His tutor had coincidentally learned that Manuel's elder and much loved brother, whom the tutor had also taught many years previously, had died six months earlier. Manuel did not see any point in speaking to anyone about his brother's death. He was insistent that while his brother's death had been a shock at the time, he had got over it now. He was certain that it had not affected his recent examination results and he attributed his lacklustre performance to a combination of other factors such as his noisy flatmates. Here we can see that the painful emotional implications of an external reality that could not be faced – the loss of a dearly loved brother – have been denied and that Manuel has not been able to move beyond the first stage of mourning for the loss of his brother.

Reaction formation is a defence in which an impulse, thought or feeling is kept from conscious awareness by invoking its opposite. For example, Susan's mother had suffered from depression for many years, in fact for most of Susan's adolescence. Susan spoke with feeling about how sorry she felt for her mother and how sad it was for her mother that she was unable to enjoy things, for example, Susan was an accomplished singer but her mother had never attended any of her performances. Her counsellor wondered if Susan had ever felt angry with her mother for not coming to hear her sing. In a shocked voice, Susan replied, 'Of course not, I love my mother!' In this case, Susan was unable to countenance the idea that she might harbour feelings of resentment towards her mother and she counteracted the counsellor's suggestion with a firm protestation of her positive feelings for her mother.

Undoing is a defence closely associated with obsessional–compulsive disorders, where an act or ritual is performed in order to undo, or cancel out, another act which has been committed in *fantasy*. This fantastical wish or act is unconscious and, being typically hostile in intent, is unacceptable to the individual. The aim of undoing is not to make good the damage done in fantasy but rather to go back in time and undo the fantasy itself. This breach with the principles of reality is plain in the magical quality of many undoing acts or rituals and is recognisable in the common act of 'touching wood' in order to undo some imagined disaster. The following example illustrates the potentially disabling effects of this defence mechanism when employed extensively. Imran, a pleasant and mild-mannered young pharmacist, had returned to university for postgraduate studies. He was a self-funding student and worked at the weekends in his local pharmacy to meet his financial needs. Since starting university however, he had become worried that he might be making mistakes and giving customers the wrong prescriptions. In an attempt to allay his escalating fears, he had contrived an elaborate system of checks and double checks including telephoning customers at home in the evening. However, his preoccupations continued to torment him and he was afraid that he might have to give up his job which would mean leaving university as he depended on the income from his job. It eventually emerged that this young man's parents had been opposed to his return to university and were impatient for him to marry. That he would have an arranged marriage had been assumed and, although he had told his parents of his wish to complete his postgraduate studies before marrying, his mother had nevertheless begun the arrangements for his marriage. While Imran appeared remarkably quiescent about his mother's plans for him, he became increasingly concerned about the harm he feared he was doing in giving incorrect prescriptions to his customers. At one level it would seem that Imran had an internal conflict between, on the one hand his desire to defy his parents (probably unconscious) and follow his own wishes, and on the other, his wish to be a dutiful son and fulfil his parents' expectations. His own attempted solution to this conflict was to return to university, thereby hopefully postponing any confrontation over his marriage. Under these circumstances, Imran's constant checking of his prescriptions could be understood as a defence against unconscious hostile impulses – stimulated by his parents' attempts to control him – which were unacceptable to him because they conflicted with his conception of himself as a loving and dutiful son.

Another mechanism of defence common in obsessional disorders is *Isolation*. Isolation protects the individual by making unconscious the logical associations connecting thoughts and/or feelings which would otherwise be experienced as painful. For example, a student complained bitterly about how difficult it was to meet with her tutor because of the limited hours he was available and the large number of students who wanted to see him. Knowing that the student had had to wait two weeks for her counselling appointment, her counsellor suggested that she might experience similar feelings of frustration with the counsellor. The student denied any such feelings and said that the two situations were completely different. In this example, we can see how the student refused to allow any link between her feelings of frustration and anger and her restricted access to her counsellor.

Identification is a psychological process that refers to the assimilation of characteristics of others and, in the course of ordinary development, it is the principal means by which the personality of the individual is constructed. Thus, for example, the person takes into themselves aspects of their parents, teachers, peers and so on and it is therefore not surprising to find that a son is like his father.

However, processes of identification can also be used in ways that inhibit rather than enrich the developing personality, as we will see in the following example. Danny was a rather shy and humourless engineering student. His dress and manner suggested an amalgam of an overly serious schoolboy and a boring middle-aged man. He was repeating his second year having failed his exams the previous year and was worried about failing again. He had been experiencing difficulties in understanding his course work and had begun to fall behind. Danny had lived away from home in his first year at university and, although it had been a rather uninspiring year both socially and academically, he had been able to extend his horizons somewhat and had enjoyed it. He had had to return to live at home during his second year for financial reasons and the long commute between university and home meant that he spent little extracurricular time at university. His father, also an engineer, had been particularly scathing of his failure and often reminded him of the extra financial burden his repeating the year had placed upon the family. The situation was exacerbated by the fact that his father faced the prospect of redundancy in the near future. Danny sometimes tried to enlist his father's help with his course work but his father was either too busy or too tired to help him. Danny described how his father would come home from a long day at work and moan at length about how unappreciated he was at work before falling asleep in front of the television. Any attempt by Danny to engage his father's interest generally met with irritation and, in the end, rejection. During his counselling sessions Danny filled the time with endless complaints about his father's lack of support and interest in him and he dismissed his counsellor's efforts to break into his monologue and open up a dialogue between them. It was clear that Danny had identified with his father lock, stock and barrel – possibly as a defence against underlying feelings of rage attendant on his father's dismissal of him – and this was evident in the re-enactment of the frustrating relationship between father and son in the counselling sessions, Danny assuming the role of his father and the counsellor being forced into the role of the useless son.

Rationalisation and *Intellectualisation* are related mechanisms of defence in that they both involve an appeal to reason at the expense of internal emotional forces. Intellectualisation, wherein ideas are entertained in the absence of their associated painful feelings, is a common defence and is particularly noticeable in students who have difficulty in establishing social relationships. Cut off from large tracts of their own potential emotional life, they often find it impossible to understand and share the emotional experiences of others. Rationalisation differs from intellectualisation in that feelings occurring as a result of internal forces may be experienced but their genesis *within* the unconscious of the individual is denied and an explanation is sought from without. For example, Sandy, a first year student, had been strongly advised to seek counselling by her friends who were concerned because she had lost a considerable amount of weight in a short space of time and was now worryingly thin. When asked if her parents knew about her recent weight loss, Sandy reported that her mother had telephoned her a few weeks ago to tell her that she and her father had decided to separate and she didn't want to bother them just now. She added that her parents had never been happy together and that a separation was probably for the best. She admitted to being surprised by her mother's announcement but didn't think it related to her recent weight loss which she attributed to the poor quality of the meals served in her student halls. Here we can see that the feelings stirred up in Sandy about her parents' separation are denied and an explanation for her weight loss is found instead in her local circumstances.

It is implicit in the foregoing discussion that paranoid–schizoid defences are, developmentally speaking, more primitive than those associated with the depressive position. While this is true in a theoretical sense, in practice the situation is usually more fluid. Generally speaking, the greater the level of anxiety that has to be managed, the stronger the tendency will be towards a paranoid–schizoid mode of function; the recent phenomenon of 'road rage' might be an example of this. Where the compulsion to act in order to relieve an intolerable level of anxiety can be resisted and the situation thought about instead, then depressive defences will tend to prevail. Let us return for a moment to the example given earlier of the insecure student who feared her ideas were being stolen from her. After the student had spoken about her paranoid fears, her counsellor suggested that perhaps she was worried that she herself might be irrevocably damaging her chances of a good degree through her current behaviour of heavy drinking, partying and non-attendance at university. The student became tearful and said that she knew she was capable of doing well but that she was afraid that she did not have enough time left now to catch up with her work. Here we can see how the student has moved from a predominantly paranoid mode of thinking, where the source of her anxieties are located outside of herself, to a more depressive style of thinking where she is more able to reflect on the damage she is doing to herself.

Homesickness

If we return to the main theme of adolescent development, namely separation, it is clear that the ability to manage loss and the attendant feelings, without either avoidance or collapse, is crucial to satisfactory progress through this stage. Losses that can be faced and worked through provide the student with a firmer foundation upon which to build. When a loss cannot be tolerated, either because of the relative emotional immaturity of the individual or because of the overwhelming nature of the loss, then paranoid–schizoid defences are more likely to emerge. The emotional impact of the loss is denied conscious access and there is therefore no opportunity to mourn the loss. Obviously, movement towards a more depressive level of functioning, where feelings about loss can be acknowledged and, hopefully, thought about, would be one aim in counselling individuals in such cases. The following two examples, both of students struggling with severe feelings of homesickness, illustrate both a successful and an unsuccessful negotiation of problems associated with loss.

Jennifer's family had recently moved from Canada to Scotland because of her father's job. Jennifer had considered staying on in Canada and attending university there but in the end decided to come to London to continue her education. She was happy with her shared university accommodation and liked her course. Her father was due to visit London in a fortnight and she herself was going to Scotland for a month over the coming Christmas vacation. Nevertheless she felt very homesick and was often weepy. She sorely missed her friends in Canada and had asked her mother if she could come to see her in Scotland the next weekend. Recognising her daughter's distress, Jennifer's mother agreed to her visit and, buoyed up by the prospect of seeing her family, Jennifer said that she would check the train times. Unfortunately rail strikes were forecast and train travel over the weekend was not advised. Upset by this set-back, Jennifer rang her mother and burst into tears. She poured out to her how isolated and lonely she felt and how she missed being with people she knew. When she had calmed down, her mother suggested two alternatives. First, if she really needed to come home then they would try and find some other means of travel, a flight or a coach perhaps; alternatively, she could arrange for Jennifer to visit some old family friends near London instead.

This family had been their neighbours for many years in Canada before they moved to England a few years ago and Jennifer remembered being very upset when they left. The idea of seeing her old neighbours again appealed to her and she told her mother that maybe it would be better if she visited them instead of trying to come home at the weekend. In her next counselling session Jennifer reported that she had had an enjoyable and relaxed weekend with these friends and had been busy back at university since. She was still missing Canada and her friends there badly and talked with sadness about the things she had had to give up to come to London. However, she also had another pressing concern, she had to find a partner for the First Year Ball. She had someone in mind but he was a little shy. A week later Jennifer said that she still felt homesick and indeed had gone to look around Canada House at the weekend. She had also had a letter from her best friend in Canada and she talked further about her mixed feelings about coming to London. However, she felt she was settling in now, she was enjoying her course and she had begun to make some new friends.

Here we can see that Jennifer is very much in touch with her feelings about leaving her home country, her family home and her friends. We might also note that this traumatic geographical move occurs in the context of Jennifer's leaving her parental home, also severely disturbed by the move, at the same time that she is starting university. Like a tree that is uprooted in a gale, she has lost many of the roots that have hitherto anchored and nourished her and she is struggling to re-establish some connections. However, despite the extent of the disruption, Jennifer manages to tolerate her feelings and continues to function at a predominantly depressive level. She remains sufficiently aware of her feelings to appreciate the extent of her losses and is also able to recognise her need for help in re-establishing new roots. She makes several attempts to deal with her feelings, some are primarily regressive and aimed at reinforcing old connections, for example, her wish to go to her mother in Scotland, her trip to Canada House, while others are indicative of an investment in her new surroundings, for example, her new friendships, and her interest in her course. Her use of the local university counselling service on the other hand can be considered both as an expression of her need to be looked after and as an indication of her capacity to find help for herself. Jennifer's account of her mother's response to her request to visit her in Scotland suggests that her mother is able to contain her daughter's homesickness in a constructive way, by acknowledging her feelings and helping her to find a way of managing them, in this instance through a visit to old family friends.

In this example, Jennifer is struggling to come to terms with intense feelings of loss and separation, not only in relation to her home country and friends but also in relation to her own childhood. Essentially she is going through a process of mourning, during the course of which, all being well, she will relinquish her childhood dependence on her parents in favour of an independence based partly upon identifications with her parents. In the following example, the experience of separation proves to be overwhelming and the student returns home.

Kathy was a very tearful first year student who had gone to university in a large city many miles from the small village in which she had grown up. Her family were all very proud of her as she was the first in the family to go to university. Her boyfriend, who worked in a local town near her village, had also been supportive of her studying away from home. During her first week she was very homesick, she hated her course and changed to a related subject. However, she continued to feel very miserable and she now thought that it wasn't so much that she was homesick – she didn't feel that she was really missing her family or boyfriend – but rather that she hated living in a city and the unstructured and sometimes chaotic student lifestyle she saw around her. Despite her mother's reservations, she went home the very next weekend. On her return she reported that the weekend had gone well and that she was much calmer and more able to think about her situation. She could now see that she had chosen her particular field of study because it provided a safe and well-structured career path and that her decision to study so far from home had been an impulsive one and represented an ill-thought out attempt to make a break from home. She had been afraid that if she had gone to a local university within easy access of her home, she would never have been able to leave home. Thus, her inability to deal with her intense ambivalence about leaving home lead to her impetuous choice of a distant university, with disastrous consequences. A week later she had decided to transfer to a university nearer to her home town.

One of the more striking features of this case is the rapidity with which Kathy reacts to her feelings, for example, her change of course of study after only one week. In contrast to Jennifer, Kathy is unable to tolerate and think about her feelings, instead she acts so as to rid herself of them as quickly as possible. Indeed, even her experience of homesickness cannot be sustained for long and her painful feelings of loss in relation to her family and boyfriend are denied and her lack of an internal capacity for containment is externalised and projected into her surroundings which she then experiences as unstructured and insufficiently containing. The observation that Kathy's distress disappears when she returns home is a further indication that she is heavily dependent on external bodies to act as containers for her feelings. Although her mother suggests she reconsider her visit home, she is unable to offer Kathy any effective alternative which may, of course, be a reflection of her mother's ambivalence about her daughter's separation from her. Following her weekend visit home Kathy feels more collected and able to consider her problems. However, although she is now able to think about the impetuosity of her choice of university as a means of avoiding her intense anxiety about leaving home, she is reluctant to explore this further and, once again, thought is eschewed in favour of action and she returns home.

In comparing these two cases of homesick students it is plain that the student's capacity to *continue to think about* their feelings was critical in determining the eventual outcome. Even though Jennifer's external circumstances were potentially more stressful than Kathy's, by virtue of the fact that she was able, with help, to remain in touch with and think about her feelings meant that she was able to successfully negotiate a number of significant losses. The development of a capacity to tolerate and think about one's feelings, in other words the internalisation of a containing relationship, was discussed at length in Chapter 2 and, as can be seen here, is crucially important in managing feelings which emerge in subsequent stages of development.

The capacity to bear separations and to mourn losses implies, to some extent, a related capability in respect of new relationships and hence, growth. This is evident in the two examples described above. Even while she is struggling with intense feelings of loss in relation to childhood friends and country, Jennifer is already putting down new roots and establishing fresh connections and a process of new growth is clearly under way. Kathy, on the other hand, cannot pull up her old roots because her anxiety about leaving home is intolerable. Unable to bear her anxiety, she returns home which inevitably reinforces her dependence on home. At the same time, her inability to manage even one weekend at university precludes any possibility of establishing new friendships at university which might otherwise help her in bearing her feelings more easily. Kathy's capacity for new growth is obviously limited and this makes it very difficult for her to move beyond the confines of what is already familiar.

It should be clear from the above examples that new growth, as opposed to an elaboration of what is already familiar, always involves separation and therefore the experience of loss and, hopefully, mourning. As discussed earlier, mourning not only clears the way for new developments, it also helps lay the foundations upon which these may be built. There are, however, many circumstances, both internal and external in origin, that may obstruct this mourning process and these will be discussed below.

Early separations

It is commonly thought that students who have had previous experience of extended periods living away from home, perhaps in boarding schools, will settle more easily into university than students leaving home for the first time. The belief underlying this presumption is that familiarity with the experience of living apart from home and family is synonymous with successful management of the feelings aroused by such separations. While this may indeed be the case for some children who have lived and studied away from home, a significant number of these children will remain emotionally unprepared for this experience on reaching university. For most children, leaving their families even temporarily stirs up some feelings of homesickness and the child's capacity to tolerate and process such feelings will depend on his relative emotional maturity. Many children respond to their detachment from home with obvious signs of depression, often becoming weepy, withdrawn and clingy, however where the child's prior attachments are reasonably secure and the new environment is sufficiently understanding and responsive to the child's feelings, this period of homesickness can be weathered. Gradually the child makes new attachments among friends and teachers and these help to compensate for the feelings of loneliness occasioned by the break with home. Clearly processes of loss and mourning are involved in the move away from home to school and, as described earlier, the capacity of the individual to tolerate the feelings involved will determine how successfully this adjustment is made. For a number of children the experience becomes unbearable and some may express their distress overtly and even demand to return home. For others, however, there may be no option of returning home, either because of family circumstances or because of their inability, or even unwillingness, to expose their unhappiness. The apparent subsequent adaptation of such children is consequentially superficial and their capacity to deal with future losses, far from being strengthened, is further compromised.

It is not unusual to find that a student who had apparently settled in without trouble several years earlier at boarding school is now unable to tolerate the subsequent shift to university. In such cases, one often finds that the painful feelings of loss accompanying the earlier separation from home have never been adequately resolved and have instead been repressed. In such cases a quasi-adaptation has been achieved at the expense of the student's learning to manage his feelings and it is this deficit that is laid bare when he is once again faced with a separation, this time occasioned by the move from school to university. Intolerable feelings about earlier separations are refreshed by this new experience of separation and, alongside the strains of moving from the relative shelter of school to the more unstructured university environment, these may prove overwhelming. The following example illustrates one such case.

Hazel had always lived in the shadow of her elder sister and despite their assertions to the contrary believed that her parents favoured her more intelligent sister. Her jealousy of her sister was the source of much of her unhappiness as a young child and when she was twelve, she pressed her parents into letting her go to boarding school. During her first year at her new school she was bullied and sometimes cried herself to sleep, however, when her parents asked how she was, she invariably told them that she was happy and enjoying school. She could not bring herself to tell them of her misery because she believed that they would have taken her out of the school and this would have meant, in her eyes, that she had failed. The following years were somewhat better in that the bullying stopped and she made a few friends among some of the other less popular girls like herself. However, despite hard work, she never excelled academically, though she did gain a place in the school swimming team which afforded her some satisfaction. She had hardly enjoyed her schooling and had been very much looking forward to coming to university where she imagined her life would blossom. However, after a few months at university she had gone to the doctor complaining that she was sleeping badly, and that she was tired and unable to concentrate on her work. Recognising that she was depressed, her doctor gently enquired whether she might be missing her family, at which Hazel broke down into sobs and continued to cry in a very desolate way for a considerable time.

In this example, we can see that Hazel's move to boarding school had been a rather desperate attempt to escape from an emotionally painful situation at home, where she felt insecure in her parents' affections. Her rejection of her parents was both an expression of her anger towards them for their apparent preference for her sister as well as a defence against her dependence on them. Her parents' acceptance, albeit reluctant, of her expressed wish to leave home possibly exacerbated an already difficult situation by compounding, in Hazel's eyes, her belief that they didn't really want her at home anyway. Hazel and her parents therefore became caught up in a dynamic whereby she mistrusted and rejected their overtures towards her, as was painfully evident in her stubborn refusal to tell them of her unhappiness at school, while they were unable or unwilling to recognise the fragile nature of their daughter's precocious independence. Far from helping her resolve her emotional problems, the move to boarding school alienated Hazel from the potential support of her family and presented her with a new set of emotional issues to deal with. It is clear from her experience at school that she felt herself to be unpopular and that she was lacking in self esteem, problems hardly dissimilar to those she had experienced while at home. It is also plain that her method of coping with her problems remained unchanged and she dealt with them in much the same way as before, by denial, and with the hope that a change in her external environment would bring relief. The inevitable disappointment that came when coming to university also failed to solve her problems appears to have been the last straw and precipitated her into a state of depression. The intensity of the loneliness and despair she felt, in part as a consequence of having cut herself off from her family, was painfully apparent in her encounter with her doctor.

Another group of young people for whom issues of separation are especially pertinent are those whose family circumstances have occasioned frequent moves. For example, children with parents employed in the diplomatic service may move country every few years, often spending the latter years in boarding school. The difficulties for these children arise from their frequent changes of home, school and friends and the protective measures that may be employed to avoid the painful feelings of repeated loss. Common defences in these circumstances include devaluation of that which has to be given up, perhaps with a concomitant idealisation of one's own resources, and avoidance of close attachments to or involvements with others. The operation of these defences can sometimes be seen to underpin problems of commitment and intimacy in relationships in later life, as in the following example.

A young man whose family had lived in a number of different countries on account of his father's business, sought help because of problems in his relationship with his girlfriend. They had met early on in their first year at university and had decided to live together during their final year. Since moving in together, however, Piers felt that his girlfriend had changed and that she had become clingy and demanding. For her part she complained that he had become cold and offhand with her. It quickly became clear that since moving in with his girlfriend he had indeed withdrawn from their relationship, often using his university work as an excuse, and that his girlfriend's expectations of greater intimacy now they were living together were experienced by him as oppressive. His history indicated a very unsettled childhood in which the family moved frequently, and rather unpredictably, in response to the vagaries of his father's business. His mother seemed to cope with this constant uprooting of her family through frantic activity, expending all of her time and energy in the practical establishment of a new home for the family while his father was tied up with making new business connections. There seemed to be no space within family life for the expression of sadness or anger about the constant upheavals in their lives although he recalled he would often comfort his younger brother when he cried. He did this by urging his brother to forget their old home and by filling his mind with exciting stories about their new home. He could not remember if he had felt sad himself when they had moved. In this account, we can see that the losses experienced by this family were not acknowledged but buried under a flurry of activity with the result that the accompanying feelings were inadequately, if at all, resolved. This failure to mourn what had been left behind meant that no internal representation of what had been lost could be established and carried forward in memory for future sustenance. While this method of avoiding pain, advocated by Piers to his brother, was effective in the short term, it was far from helpful in the longer term. The two main problems were that it deprived Piers of a valuable cache of experience upon which to draw in the future and that it further weakened his capacity to face his feelings in response to future loss. The extent of Piers' anxiety in this respect was evident in his current problem with his girlfriend. His girlfriend's wish to get emotionally closer during their final year together at university, with the strong likelihood that they might separate for further studies thereafter, threatened him with the very situation that he had striven to avoid all his life, namely attachment followed by loss. Of course, because of his enormous deprivation in this respect, a part of him yearned to be close and this caused a conflict because to give in to this longing would make him vulnerable. It seems that one way in which he managed this conflict was by making use of projective identification. Thus, his desire for intimacy was projected into others and experienced as belonging to them – it was others who shed tears and felt pain at loss and who were clingy and demanding and wished to be close, not he. We can also see how he attempted to master these disavowed aspects of himself in the other, for example, by inducing his brother to forget his losses and look to the future. The situation with his girlfriend was complicated by her resistance to his projections. She did not accept his negative interpretation of her wish for greater intimacy, seeing it rather as an appropriate progression in their relationship. As a result of this he was forced further in the direction of the conflict he was struggling to avoid.

Students like Hazel and Piers, who deal with repeated experiences of loss principally through the use of mechanisms such as denial and projective identification, often find it difficult to explore their feelings in counselling because of overt or covert fears of becoming depressed. While psychological defences should always be respected, this is particularly the case with such students in whom an apparent 'togetherness' may be masking a severe underlying depression. In such cases it is important to assess what support the student has and, if necessary, to consider ways of bolstering this. These students commonly fail to attend or keep up counselling appointments and this can be understood on a number of levels, for instance as a defence against becoming aware of painful feelings, as an expression of their futility about the permanence of relationships, as an enactment of their feelings of rejection, and so on.

For the majority of students, the losses that accompany the transition from home to university are adequately compensated for by new experiences and a growing sense of independence. If the demands of the new environment are experienced as excessive, however, then the positive feelings consequent upon increased mastery of one's life will be replaced by negative feelings and a sense of inadequacy and failure may take hold. It will be clear from the foregoing discussion that the capacity of each individual student to tolerate and adapt successfully to university will depend, to a considerable extent, on their particular previous experiences. However, as briefly mentioned at the start of this chapter, there are a number of external factors which may adversely affect the student's ability to settle in at university. Most pertinent to today's students are the changes in the level of financial support provided by the state and the uncertainty about future employment after graduation. In both cases there has been an attrition in the sense of security previously afforded to students alongside a greatly increased expectation upon individuals to provide for themselves. The rapid expansion in the number of individuals entering higher education in recent years has not been accompanied by a commensurate financial input from government and this has resulted in a relative decrease in state funded resources in the form of grants available to support each individual student. In order to meet the financial shortfall between their student grant and loan and their living expenses while at university, many students take up part-time jobs alongside their studies. This relative shift from financial dependence on the state to greater dependence on parental contributions or personal earnings can have varying effects. For those individuals who are fortunate and are able to find and take on reasonably paid work in addition to their studies, the necessity of having to contribute to their education, if not excessive, may enhance their sense of independence and help to prepare them for working life after university. However, for many students, the experience is one of poorly paid work that leaves insufficient time for studies alongside an increased dependence on parents who may resent the additional financial demand or who may not be in a position to help out. Thus, the relative loss of financial independence afforded by more adequate student grants in previous years, fosters continued dependence on the family and further complicates the individual's struggle to separate from home and family.

Further reading

Bowlby, J. (1969) *Attachment and Loss, vol.1, Attachment,* London: Hogarth.

Bowlby, J. (1973) *Attachment and Loss, vol.2, Separation,* London: Hogarth.

Bowlby, J. (1980) *Attachment and Loss, vol.3, Loss,* London: Hogarth.

Freud, A. (1936) *The Ego and the Mechanisms of Defence,* London: Hogarth.

Rutter, M. (1972) *Maternal Deprivation Reassessed,* Harmondsworth: Penguin.

Segal, H. (1973) *Introduction to the Work of Melanie Klein,* London: Hogarth.

Waddell, M. (1998) *Inside Lives: Psychoanalysis and the Growth of the Personality,* London: Duckworth.

4

FAMILIES AND THE TIES
THAT BIND

In Chapter 3 we examined the importance of the individual's personal history of separation and loss in shaping their subsequent experience of leaving home and starting university. It is clear that exposure to repeated losses, before adequate resources have been developed to manage the painful feelings engendered, can lead to the precocious establishment of a defensive structure whose foundations are insufficiently robust to deal with the emotional demands of subsequent developments. We also looked briefly at the pressures upon students occasioned by the decrease in financial support from the state in recent years. In this chapter we will examine another potential source of conflict that may beset the student struggling to settle in at university, namely their family.

Family dynamics

Families amount to more than the sum of their individual parts. Each family evolves a unique structure and dynamic system whose unwritten, and largely unacknowledged, rules govern the lives of its members. The needs of the family unit and those of the individuals who compose it are occasionally coincident, at which times harmony prevails, but more often than not there is some degree of conflict. While the complete absence of friction within the family might appear to represent an ideal state of affairs, it is hardly more conducive to the long-term well being of the family and its constituents than a state of permanent strife. The well-functioning family requires periods of both concord and discord in order that its members can pursue their emotional development fully. The role of the family, therefore, is not to maintain itself unchanged and unchallenged, but rather to provide an environment which is sufficiently frustrating, but not overwhelmingly so, to be conducive to the growth and development of its members, and to prepare them for their eventual independence from the family. Inevitably, conflicts arise between the demands of the individual and the needs of the family as a whole and these threaten the integrity and functioning of the family as a system. Most families experience crises of this sort, where one or other family member asserts their independence at the expense of the family as a whole, as for example when a teenager who is too young to be left at home refuses to go on family holidays. In such an event there are many possible responses the family can make in response to this conflict. For example, a younger child may become ill, thereby shifting the focus of concern from his older sibling and, if he is ill enough, the conflict may be resolved by cancellation of the holiday. Alternatively, a father may try to enforce accord by exercising his authority over the family, with scant regard for the child's wishes, and insist that the child comes along. A couple with little sense of their parental responsibilities may deal with the conflict by ignoring it and simply leave their unwilling child unattended at home. These are extreme solutions and indicate rigid family structures that cannot accommodate challenge and find compromises but rather are driven to action to resolve conflict. For the family that can tolerate some dissension, however, there comes the possibility of negotiation which takes into account the needs of all the family members. In the example described here, this may take a relatively primitive form such as cajoling and offering inducements or may be of a more mature order and include an appeal to the child's reason or a discussion about alternative arrangements with the child. A family that is responsive and can adjust in respect of the evolving needs of its members is more likely to survive intact and be available to continue in its task of supporting its members. However, in order to continue to function in this sensitive fashion, the family requires a certain minimum level of cooperation and support from its members. When this is unforthcoming as, for example, the child who refuses outright to join a family holiday, the family may feel driven for instance towards diversionary action through the sickness of another family member, authoritarian imposition of the father's will or in the direction of a dereliction of parental responsibilities.

The needs of the individual and the 'Oedipus complex'

The flexibility of the family system is therefore of considerable importance, both in ensuring its own survival and in maintaining its capacity to accommodate the demands of its individual members. The anxiety attendant on the family's ability in respect of these two tasks is amply evident when the family is faced with unexpected and possibly unwelcome news, for instance, the intense fear that prevents a son from informing his parents of his homosexuality, the terror experienced by a daughter with an unplanned pregnancy or the shame and anger felt by a fifty-five year old man forced into redundancy. In each case, the individual fears that their family will not be able to accept and tolerate them as they now are and that they will be punished or rejected for letting the family down and for failing to fulfil their family's, often unstated, expectations of them. That they may also share these expectations of themselves both complicates and adds to the pain of the situation. Where anxiety about the family's response is intense, splitting mechanisms are more likely to prevail and that which is potentially good in the family, namely its capacity to provide understanding, tolerance and support, is likely to be 'forgotten'. Where an extreme family response is predicted – 'It would kill my parents if they found out!' – it is more likely that this is indicative of severe splitting by the individual than that it is an accurate reflection of the state of affairs at home (which is not to say that there are not families who do respond in very harsh ways). There are a number of different factors, such as financial circumstances; ill health, particularly if chronic; support available from extended family and community; and so on which influence the relative flexibility of the family, at any given time, in its response to events that tax it. For example, the family whose main breadwinner has been made unexpectedly redundant would be hard pressed to respond sympathetically to their eldest son's news that he has failed his exams and wants to repeat the year, especially if they have to pay his fees for the repeated year.

The continued integrity of the family is especially important to the young person engaged in the task of leaving it. If relationships at home have been reasonably happy, then some sadness all round is inevitable at the passing of this stage in the life of the family. Adequate compensations help in mitigating the pain of the loss to the family, for example, parents may gain more time for themselves as well as satisfaction in the progress of their child, while siblings may benefit from more space at home and sometimes come out of the shadow of an older brother or sister. For the would-be student, it is important that their family survive their departure in good shape, not only to ease the sense of guilt occasioned through identification with those left behind but also because of their own continuing need for a home to return to, both in times of emotional crises and during holidays. Parents who have put off their own needs, perhaps to end an unhappy marriage, may wait until their children leave home to go to university believing that their children no longer need them. Sometimes the decision to split up has been made some time before but not discussed with the children for fear of upsetting them before important exams. Under these circumstances both parents and children may experience the other as thoughtless in respect of their needs. Parents who have silently persevered in an unhappy home situation 'for the sake of the children' may believe that they have done enough while their children may feel let down at a time when there is already so much change in their lives without the unforeseen break up of their family to contend with. Even where discord between parents has been obvious and their eventual separation unsurprising, children are often shocked and disbelieving. This apparent blindness in respect of the state of their parents' relationship can be understood in terms of defensive denial and provides the child with a powerful protection from an emotionally painful reality, namely the destruction of their parents' relationship.

But why should the preservation of a perhaps acrimonious parental relationship be so important to the child? There are a number of different factors which together contribute towards a child's anxiety about the breakdown of his parents' relationship. Significant among these is the child's fear that one or other of his parents will be unable to cope on their own and that he will have to step into the breach. The task of having to comfort a bereft and depressed parent, or console a rageful betrayed one, can be overwhelming. A second factor, related to the fear that they may be unable to withstand, let alone ameliorate, their parents' feelings, is the anxiety that they may not be able to manage their own feelings in relation to their parents' separation. A third complicating factor arises out of the shattering of the child's fantasy of an ideal parental couple. The child's wish for parents out of whose *loving* union he was created is a powerful one and the shortcomings of reality are often made good through fantasy. Thus, in the face of obvious enmity between his parents, a child may retreat from reality into fantasy and the belief that his parents love each other and will remain together. Associated with the child's reluctance to admit the hostility between his parents is a fourth factor which pertains to the vagaries of the child's rivalrous relations with his parents during a particular stage of his or her development (often referred to as the *Oedipus complex* and posited as occurring at an age of around three to five years). Essentially, the developmental tasks facing the child during this phase involve the resolution of feelings arising out of largely unconscious wishes to possess the parent of the opposite sex and to get rid of the parent of the same sex. Such feelings are commonly evident in young children's statements in which they may openly express a wish to marry mummy or daddy when they grow up and often have distant echoes in their subsequent choice of spouse. For example, people are frequently surprised when quite obvious similarities between a partner and a parent are pointed out to them. The usual outcome of this developmental stage is for the child to give up his opposite sex parent as the object of his desires and transfer these to a more suitable, and often similar, figure *and* to identify with the same sex parent who had previously been his rival. Put simply, for a boy, this would take the form of wanting to marry someone *like* his mother and to grow up into a man like his father. However, to return to the issue of the child's anxiety about the breakdown of his parents' relationship, it follows that this is in fact an outcome that every child has, sometimes consciously, wished for at some time in his or her life. That children commonly feel responsible when their parents separate, often with little apparent justification, suggests that this fulfilment of their old desire stirs up associated feelings of guilt. The experience of guilt in relation to one's fantasies is a common phenomenon and will be familiar to people, for example, in the ambivalent emotions that follow a bereavement. There are, therefore, complex historical factors underpinning a child's unwillingness to acknowledge the breakdown of his parents' relationship.

Plainly there are circumstances when parental separation is desired by all parties, including the children, however, most situations are less clear cut. Communications between separating parents are typically poor and acrimonious with children often feeling caught up in the crossfire. Such circumstances promote splitting and paranoid attitudes and cooperation and flexibility are difficult to maintain. The formation of new relationships, by either parent, at this stage further complicates the emotional picture and children may feel confused and torn in their loyalties. It can be especially painful for a student if their parent establishes a new sexual relationship with someone of an age similar to them. This scenario carries clear resonances with the Oedipal situation and the following example illustrates some of the problems that may arise when feelings associated with this developmental phase are so directly aroused. Jodie had always been close to her father and though she generally kept out of arguments between her parents and appreciated that there was fault on both sides, her sympathies lay more often with him. She had little time for her mother's frequent complaints about her father and considered her mother's demands for him to spend more time with her 'pathetic'. However, when her father's year long affair with a woman of her own age was discovered by her mother and Jodie shortly after she had started at university, Jodie's allegiances shifted dramatically and her adored father became 'the villain' in the family. In contrast to her previous avoidance of her, Jodie began to spend more time at home with her mother, promoting and supporting her outpourings against her father. Jodie's new-found sympathy for her mother indicated a number of underlying dynamics including conscious and unconscious identifications with her mother in their joint betrayal by her father. Also, her encouragement of her mother in her vilification of her father suggested that she was using her mother, probably unconsciously, as a means of expressing her own rage at her father's betrayal. In this case Jodie responded to the crisis in her family precipitated by her father's affair with an efflorescence of splitting and projective identification mechanisms. She pressed her mother to force her father to leave the family home and, when her mother expressed reluctance in this direction, Jodie left university and returned home herself. Her father did eventually leave and Jodie resumed her university studies the following year. While this is, of course, an extreme case, it serves to illustrate the intensity of the unconscious feelings associated with the Oedipal stage of development as well as the powerful effect of the defences that may be erected to keep such feelings at bay. This example also demonstrates how such defences, when used extensively, promote rigidity and militate against discussion and flexibility of response. There was never any question of Jodie's parents' seeking counselling for themselves and indeed Jodie herself was disinclined to exploring *her* feelings about her father's affair. From the outset it was clear that her preference, albeit unconscious, was for a battle between her parents in which she could find an outlet for her own unconscious feelings.

Clearly the capacity to think about, rather than act impulsively upon, feelings is a critical factor in determining the available options. In families where feelings cannot be faced or sufficiently restrained to allow exploration of alternative ways of managing them, as in the example above, access to potential solutions can become severely restricted. In the following two examples, the more open and flexible response of one family is in marked contrast to the rigid reaction of the other and this difference is reflected in the subsequent expansion and contraction, respectively, of the developmental possibilities of the students described in the two cases.

In the summer before starting university Melanie had numerous arguments with her mother about her accommodation for the coming year. Her mother had wanted her to go into university-managed accommodation for her first year at least. Melanie was her only child and, having given up a promising career in advertising in order to look after her while she was at school, she had found it difficult to adjust to her daughter's growing independence of her and was concerned about her future. Nevertheless, and partly in preparation for her daughter's imminent departure, a year previously Melanie's mother had begun a small and relatively successful business selling dried flowers and she had plans to expand this business when Melanie left home. Melanie had always considered her mother to be over-protective and she now experienced her mother's caution and concern about her wish to move into a flat with people she hardly knew as entirely unreasonable and restrictive. She had appealed to her father who had himself shared a flat with fellow students during his time at university. Caught between his wife and daughter, her father had tried to reach a compromise but in the end Melanie got her own way and started her first term living in a shared flat. Having reached the end of her second term at university she had come to the unhappy realisation that she hated living in shared accommodation, mainly because of the inconsiderate behaviour, as she saw it, of her three flatmates. She complained that the other girl in their flat borrowed her clothes without asking, that the two boys ate her food, again without her permission, and that none of them would help with keeping the flat clean and tidy. She had tried in various ways to change their behaviour, she had cajoled and nagged and even drawn up a rota of household tasks, all without success. Her intense efforts to curb the wayward behaviour of her flatmates had clear echoes in her descriptions of her mother's attempts to control her and she showed the same intolerance and irritation when frustrated in this task as she had described in her mother. When the close similarity between herself and her mother in this respect was mentioned to her, she was dismissive and, to prove her point, she provided further instances of her flatmates' bad behaviour. There was no question in her mind but that her flatmates were at fault. The thought of a third term with them was intolerable to her, she was unable to concentrate on her course work and was already worried about her end of year exams. She wanted to move into student halls but could not leave the flat because she had paid three terms rent in advance and could certainly not afford another rent on top. When her counsellor wondered whether her parents might be able to help her out, Melanie said that she had not told her parents about how unhappy she was. She said that they would say that she had made her bed and now she must lie on it. It was clear that she did not expect a sympathetic response from them, rather that having disregarded their helpful advice, she expected them to retaliate, along the lines of 'serves you right'. Plainly she was still caught up in a struggle for independence with her parents, especially with her mother, in the light of which to ask for help was tantamount to admitting defeat. From Melanie's point of view, she had rejected her parents and she expected a harsh reaction from them. She had projected her own intolerant attitude, as displayed in her lack of patience with her flatmates and in her immediate dismissal of her counsellor's suggestion, onto her parents and expected little understanding from them. The final straw came when, having returned to the flat late one evening, she found her jar of coffee empty. Unable to contain her rage and frustration any longer, she burst into tears and rang her mother. Her mother listened patiently for almost an hour as she poured out her bitter complaints, then suggested that she come home at the weekend to talk things over. While Melanie was unsure whether her parents would agree to pay for her to move into halls, she was certain that they would let her know how foolish she had been. To her surprise, her parents listened sympathetically to her and, after a discussion about her options, agreed to pay for her to go into student halls for her third term. As she put it, 'They treated me like an adult!'

In this example we can see that Melanie's struggle for control with her mother is central to the family dynamics and indeed, it is this same dynamic, carried over into her relationships with her flatmates, that continues to bedevil her at university. While it sounds likely that Melanie's mother was overly controlling of her, there is also evidence to suggest that her mother had begun to accept her daughter's eventual departure in her reinvestment of her energies in a new business. In the light of their response to her problem, Melanie's anxiety that turning to her parents for help would herald a return to her position as a dependent child was indicative of her ambivalence about her independence. Her family had, in fact, already adjusted to her increasing need for independence.

The impact of external circumstances and events upon the family is unquestionable, less obvious is the critical influence exerted through unconscious dynamics within the family. The following example demonstrates the potentially harmful effect of unresolved feelings from the past upon the present life of the family.

Graham was half way through the second year of his pharmacy course when his girlfriend, Parveen, told him that she was pregnant. They had met at university and had been together for just over a year. Neither had any clear plans for the future, though Graham had thought he might like to go on to postgraduate studies. Parveen was determined to continue the pregnancy and to keep the baby despite knowing that her family would certainly offer no support and might even disown her. Graham was much less clear in his thinking and was struggling to resolve highly conflictual feelings. On the one hand, although neither of them harboured long-term plans for their relationship, he was fond of Parveen and wanted to support her wishes, especially as it seemed unlikely that her family would be of much help. On the other hand he did not want to become a father at this stage in his life, he did not feel ready for such responsibilities yet. However, if Parveen had the baby then he knew that he could not just wash his hands of it. He was also very aware of how severely his role as a father would restrict whatever plans he might have for his own future. The following week Graham went home to discuss the situation with his parents. Although they were not an emotionally close family, his parents had been generally supportive of him in the past and he had always regarded them as fair minded. He had not expected them to be thrilled to learn that they were to become grand-parents, however, the strength of their response shocked him, especially his father's reaction. His father accused Parveen of becoming pregnant deliberately in order to force Graham to marry her and he urged Graham to have nothing more to do with her or her baby. While Graham's mother did not share her husband's suspiciousness in this respect, she was nevertheless opposed to her son's becoming any further involved with Parveen whom she did not regard as a suitable addition to their family. His father's paranoid hostility and his mother's barely disguised racist attitude towards his girlfriend deeply shook him. On returning to his flat, he rang his elder sister who was not surprised by his account of his recent visit home. She told him that their parents had married because their mother was pregnant and that she had suffered a miscarriage a month after the wedding. Neither of their families had approved of the match nor had they supported the couple and there had been a great deal of bad feeling all round when the baby was lost. His sister had asked their mother if she regretted marrying their father and she had replied simply: 'Well, we were never in love or anything like that.' Graham and Parveen eventually decided that he would complete his second year and that he would then take a year out to support her and return to complete his degree the following year. On hearing his decision, his parents withdrew their financial contribution to his studies and Graham was forced to work part-time while he completed his second year. His sister tried to intervene on his behalf, but without success.

It is clear that Graham had unconsciously recreated the traumatic circumstances of his parents' marriage. Their intense reaction suggested that his parents had not been able to deal satisfactorily with their feelings about their own predicament many years ago and had instead repressed them only to have them re-evoked by their son's situation. His mother's rather terse response to his sister's question implied that his parents' relationship had been lacking in romantic love, possibly a source of bitterness for both of them, while his father's acute hostility towards Parveen may have been an echo of his having felt trapped into marrying Graham's mother. That Graham had not been consciously aware of the unhappy circumstances of his parents' marriage until he spoke to his sister indicated that such matters were probably not discussed openly within the family. Further support for this view came from his parents' wish that he cut Parveen out of his life completely, thereby indicating their continuing unwillingness to face any painful feelings stirred up in them by the events of Parveen's pregnancy. The extent of his parents' intransigence became clear when, against their wishes, Graham elected to take a year out and involved himself further with Parveen. This was, of course, a partial repetition of his parents' 'solution' to their problem of an unplanned pregnancy and was possibly the last straw for them.

The inflexibility of this family and their inability to accommodate their conflicting needs finally led to the break up of the family. This case also serves to illustrate the potentially destructive power of unconscious processes, in this instance the parents' projective identification with their son and his girlfriend.

The needs of the family

In the previous section the needs of the individual as opposed to those of the family were discussed and in this section the demands that the family makes upon the individual will be explored. However, before we do so, it should be borne in mind that the real situation is rarely as clear cut as this implies and more often there is a subtle interplay between the pressures each party exerts on the other. For example, Melanie's mother's redirection of her interests into her new business the year before Melanie left home, as well as being a positive adaptation to her daughter's independence, could also be understood as a retaliatory rejection of her daughter, in which case Melanie's subsequent dismissal of her mother's concern might be construed as a response in kind, and so on. Given this inherent complexity, the task of gauging the appropriate level at which to address a current situation requires careful judgment and is a central element in the counselling process. A further complicating factor is the cultural context of the family. The demands of families are, to a significant degree, culturally determined and expectations within families vary according to the mores of their culture. For example, in Japanese families the needs and wishes of the individual are considered secondary to those of the family as a group. Given the increasing number of students choosing to study in foreign countries, sensitivity to such cultural differences is particularly important. With these caveats in mind, we may turn our attention to the demands that families impose upon their individual members.

That children make taxing demands upon their families, sometimes exceeding what can be borne by their family, is generally recognised and accepted as one of the challenges of parenthood. Less well articulated, however, are the demands that families may make upon their children. These demands may be conscious and either explicit or implicit, for example, a young man may be studying law at his father's old university because his father has insisted he do so; or they may be unconscious, for example, a promising French student who unexpectedly failed her exams and was therefore unable to go on her year abroad was responding to an unconscious communication from her widowed and isolated mother to stay at home. Of course, the individual may be more or less aware of the demands being made on them. The law student was in no doubt as to his father's expectations of him while the French student was not conscious of any connection between her exam failure and her mother's fears of being left alone. In the following example, the demands of the family are fairly explicit, however, their damaging effect on the emotional life of the individual concerned is not recognised.

Ashok, a medical student, came to see a counsellor in the third term of his second year. He had fallen badly behind with his work and thought it likely that he would fail his end of year exams. He was drinking more heavily than usual, which made it hard to get up in the morning and he had missed several lectures through sleeping in. His drinking had increased because the 'rock' band that he had played in since leaving school had become moderately successful as a result of which he was often at gigs or rehearsals in local pubs during the week. He had found his first year studying medicine relatively easy and had managed to scrape through his exams by cramming at the last minute. This year had been more exacting and he had been struggling to keep up with his work at the same time as fulfilling his commitments with the band. He was particularly concerned about what his parents would say if he failed the year. His parents owned a small supermarket and it was assumed that his elder brother would eventually take this over. Unlike his brother and younger sister, Ashok had not been expected to help out in the family shop. Rather, being designated 'the clever one' in the family who would go on to university, his parents considered that he needed the time after school for homework. Ashok could not remember with any clarity where the idea that he should study medicine had come from and thought that perhaps his parents or a teacher had suggested it to him. It was clear that Ashok had passively accepted the role allotted to him within his family and that his growing interest in music conflicted with this. He had no thoughts about his future career in medicine other than that his mother had told friends and relations that he was studying to become a GP and he was unable to talk about his future except in terms of what his parents wanted. On the few occasions when he had tried to talk to his parents about his lack of interest in medicine, his mother became acutely distressed and his father called him self-ish and blamed him for upsetting his mother. His brother and sister, who resented their parents' preferential treatment of him, were unsympathetic. Ashok did in fact fail his exams and his parents, who had hitherto accepted his involvement in music, insisted that he leave the band to concentrate on studying for his resits which he duly passed. In the following year he became severely depressed and was considered too unwell to complete the year. He left university with the option of returning the following year.

In this example it is plain that Ashok occupied a central role in his family where his mother's desire for a doctor in the family came before everyone else's needs, including his. His family structure proved to be rigid and unable to adjust to accommodate the conflict between his wishes and those of his mother. Unable to acknowledge, let alone assert, his needs in the face of his mother's wishes, and lacking support from his father or siblings, Ashok's unconscious rage at his mother's disregard for his needs was redirected inwards and he became depressed. Of course, through this unconscious route he did in fact defy his mother, however, his victory was a Pyrrhic one and the cost to both himself and his family was enormous.

The next example illustrates how the further development of one member of a family threatened to destroy the family. Craig was from a close-knit family who lived in the far north of Scotland. He had been one of twins, his twin sister having died from a childhood illness when he was three years old. His parents had been unsuccessful in their attempts to have more children and Craig described himself as 'an only child'. Throughout his childhood he had kept several pets and his strong interest in animals was evident in his choosing to study veterinary medicine. His parents were thrilled when he was accepted for a prestigious veterinary school in the south of England. After a period of homesickness Craig eventually settled in and by the end of his first term was enjoying university life. He returned home for the Christmas vacation and though his parents were very pleased to see him, he had found the atmosphere at home strained. A couple of weeks after his return to university, his father, a building surveyor, fell from a ladder, badly damaging his back. The doctors were unsure when, if at all, he would be fit for work again. A hardworking man, his father found convalescing at home difficult. His mother, who did not work outside the home, complained about having his father under her feet all day. In particular, she found his anger and frustration on account of his helplessness, frightening. Ordinarily a timid woman, her husband's outbursts unnerved her and after a series of minor household accidents, the family doctor prescribed a minor tranquiliser to 'steady her nerves'. Meanwhile, Craig had begun to lose interest in his university life and was increasingly preoccupied with the situation at home where his parents were clearly not coping. His mother often broke down in tears when they spoke on the phone, which he found particularly difficult to deal with. He began to return home more frequently and, because of the long distance, often extended his visits beyond the weekend. By the end of the second term he had fallen irredeemably behind and, on the advice of his tutor, he withdrew from the course. While Craig's family did not ostensibly begin to disintegrate until his father's accident at work, their subsequent response in the face of the problems this threw up suggested that the family had been unable to accommodate the significant changes to its basic structure occasioned by his departure for university. Thus, with the integrity of the family weakened by the 'loss' of their son to university, which probably stirred up painful feelings about their much earlier loss of his twin, his parents were unable to sustain the further damage to the family as a result of Craig's father's accident. In addition, Craig's apparent lack of ambivalence about leaving his course, which he had been enjoying, in order to return home to support his parents suggested that anxiety about the state of his family pre-empted any considerations about his own independent development. Under the circumstances, his parents' immediate acquiescence with his decision to leave university and return home most likely served to confirm his anxieties.

In both these examples, demands from home, whether explicit or implicit, were central to the young person's failure at university. Neither family was sufficiently flexible to be able to tolerate, let alone support, the autonomous development of one of its members outside of the family. Ashok's education was, essentially, geared towards satisfying his mother's needs, while Craig's move to university was, ultimately, compromised because of his parents' inability to cope without him.

As discussed at the beginning of this chapter, all families comprise of interactive systems, one consequence of which is that activity in one part of the system is very likely to have repercussions in other parts of the system. Families are complex systems in which there may be many subsystems depending on both the extent of the family network and the contact between members. The potential array of relationships thus afforded may be experienced positively as a source of support and pleasure as well as negatively, perhaps as meddlesome and unwelcome. For example, responses to a proposed family visit at half term are likely to vary considerably. While some students are happy for their families to meet their new university friends and to see where they live, others experience such interest on the part of their family as grossly intrusive. The majority of students fall somewhere between these two groups and display a more openly ambivalent relationship to their family. As already indicated, families are complex systems and a fuller understanding of the emotional dynamics underlying these systems is beyond the remit of this book. (There is an extensive literature on family dynamics and family therapy and readers interested in further study in this area are directed to the introductory references at the end of this chapter.) However, one factor contributing to the flexibility of both the family system and its constituent members, is the degree to which relationships within the family are characterised by projective identification. As discussed earlier, this mechanism functions to protect the individual from becoming aware of painful thoughts or feelings by disowning them in himself and relocating them, so to speak, in another. While most individuals use projective identification in this way at times, its prevalence as a defence mechanism tends to recede with increased emotional maturity and the availability of other defences. Thus, a four year old whose mother is upstairs having a bath, on hearing a strange noise in the house, might hug his dog tightly and say, 'Don't worry, mummy will be down soon.' Here the child is using projective identification to help him manage fears which might otherwise, on account of his young age and relative vulnerability, become over-whelming. They are projected into his dog whom he is then able to comfort and reassure. However, when a nineteen year old girl with very low self esteem tells her tutor that she wants to leave university after only one week because everyone is talking about her behind her back, we see how projective identification may be used in a manner which is damaging. Here the girl's intensely negative feelings about herself are projected into her fellow students who are then perceived by her as thinking ill of her. Her misperceptions cause her to with-draw even further from the other students whom she experiences as rejecting and malevolent.

As with all unconscious mechanisms, projective identification militates against open communication and discussion and in fami-lies where it is used extensively, severely restricts their creative possibilities. For example, in Ashok's family, his mother's *personal* ambitions, clearly discernible in her remarks to friends and rela-tions, were disavowed and projected into Ashok who acted as if they were his own, albeit unenthusiastically. Unsurprisingly, serious problems arose when they came into conflict with his own wishes. If his family had been more able to take responsibility for their own feelings, then it might have been possible for Ashok and his parents to talk about and find alternative and more constructive ways of meeting their respective needs.

Evolving family structures

The traditional family unit comprising of mother, father and their biological children, has given over considerable ground in recent years to newer structures which have grown up primarily in the wake of increasing divorce rates but also as a consequence of greater social tolerance for alternative family structures. Single parent families, step-families and families where both parents are of the same sex, are becoming more common. The ramifications of these developments for children in these families are complex and their proper investigation is beyond the scope of this book. However, observation of students from single parent and step-families allows for some general remarks. Students who effectively have one parent, typically their mother, often describe a close knit family structure which may be reflected in frequent visits home and, not infrequently, problems in maintaining close relationships outside of the family. For these students, their mother's or father's lack of a satisfactory long lasting relationship may be perceived, perhaps at an unconscious level, as a 'deficiency' and as such, may make it more difficult for them to leave their parent at home alone. It may also foster an underlying anxiety about their own capacity for long term relationships. This is less likely to be the case where their parent's relationships with friends and family are secure and stable and thereby afford an ultimate sense of optimism about relationships. In addition to these more transparent emotional issues, there are likely to be any number of unconscious ideas that might prove troublesome – feelings of resentment, for instance, are often deeply buried in single parent families and their emergence strongly guarded against, especially if the family is felt to be fragile. Thus, a teenager who is struggling to establish a more secure sense of himself can risk diverting and expressing some of his confused feelings through hurtful remarks towards his mother provided that she has someone, usually her husband, to help her bear her son's ingratitude and criticisms. The child whose mother (or father) lacks support of this kind has less emotional freedom and may be more inclined to protect his parent from his destructive impulses by repressing them. The following example illustrates potential difficulties that may arise as a result of such unconscious feelings.

Eleanor had been going out with her boyfriend, Dan, for six months when they decided to live together. They had got on well in their first year and thought that they might enjoy sharing a flat together in their second year at university. However, within a week of living together they were arguing over the slightest things. Eleanor described one such row from the previous morning. She had made a cup of coffee and discovered there was no milk left in the fridge although there had been a full pint the night before. She woke Dan who explained that he had been thirsty in the night and had drunk the milk. He apologised and offered to get up and fetch some. By way of response, Eleanor accused him of being selfish and of never thinking about her needs. Dan said that he did not think it such a big issue and repeated that he would go and get more milk but Eleanor continued to berate him until she eventually burst into tears. Later, when she had calmed down she could not understand why she had become so worked up over a drop of milk. Some information about Eleanor's family background helped make things clearer. Eleanor was the eldest of three children in a one-parent family, her father had left soon after the twins were born, around the time she was four years old. Her mother had had a few relationships since but none lasting beyond a few months. When the twins started school, Eleanor's mother went back to work and it fell to Eleanor to pick the twins up from school and look after them until her mother came home. Looking after the twins and helping her mother at home took up a lot of her free time. Although she sometimes missed not being able to spend more time with her school friends, she was well aware of how hard things were for her mother and she never considered asking if she could have more time for herself. However, when she applied for university, Eleanor was clear that she wanted to live away from home, with no one to think about but herself. And indeed she had enjoyed her first year living in university halls very much.

In the light of this information about her family circumstances, we can begin to discern some of the possible dynamics underlying Eleanor's outbursts against her boyfriend. At one level, her outbursts could be understood in terms of the eruption of repressed, and therefore unconscious, feelings of jealousy and resentment in relation to the needs of her twin sisters coming before her own when she was younger. The emergence of such feelings at this point in her life now was probably linked to moving in with her boyfriend and the increased commitment in their relationship that this represented. For Eleanor, close relationships meant putting the other person's feelings before her own, as she had done for years with her mother and the twins, and this dynamic was revitalised when she moved in with Dan. Of course, her father's abandonment of the family was another significant factor and buried feelings of disappointment and anger at his lack of concern for her may also have found expression in her outbursts towards Dan when, in her mind, he echoed her father's negligent attitude and let her down. In other words, Eleanor's relationship with Dan was permeated with unconscious aspects of her relationships with her parents.

A significant proportion of the problems that beset children whose parents form new relationships after separating can be understood in terms of the consequent changes in their family structure, especially those which impinge directly on their relationships with their (biological) parents. Such changes provoke considerable uncertainty and therefore anxiety. Under these circumstances splitting mechanisms become more prevalent and blame and accusation tend to prevail. The 'wicked step-mother/father' is often perceived as responsible for the destruction of the parental relationship as well as a threat to the child's relationships with his parents, even in situations where the parents have been apart for some time. In this latter case, it may be the child's fantasy of the parents coming together again, or an idealised memory of the parental partnership, that feels under threat. The more anxious and insecure the child feels, the more likely he is to resort to splitting as a means of dealing with his feelings. A parent who is caught up in the excitement of a new relationship may minimise or fail to notice their children's misgivings about the new situation unless these are brought forcibly to their attention, for example, if problems at school are reported. This lack of sensitivity is more problematic where children are about to leave or have recently left home to study since their anxieties are more likely to pass unrecognised because of the literal separation between the student and his 'new' family.

Students who experience their mother/father's new relationship as excluding and rejecting of them may react in many different ways. Some may respond with overt symptoms of depression. They may lose interest in work and friends, feel irritable and oversensitive to criticism and suffer from minor illnesses. They may feel as though there is no point to anything anymore. Students who have had a close and possibly exclusive relationship with the parent who has established a new relationship are particularly prone to respond in this way. Other students may respond with more obvious signs of anxiety and insecurity, becoming more demanding and clinging in their relationships with their peers, as though afraid of being abandoned. In contrast to these individuals are those students who defend themselves against feelings of rejection by means of reaction formation. In the following example, we can see how one student protected himself from becoming aware of potentially painful feelings in relation to his mother's new relationship by invoking their opposite. Greg had been his mother's close confidante and supporter throughout the turbulent years that had preceded her eventual separation from his violent father. Not long after Greg started university, his mother began a relationship with an old friend of her ex-husband, a man who was aggressive and short-tempered like Greg's father. When asked how he felt about his mother's new relationship, Greg had replied, 'Its great! He's a great bloke.' Greg's response to his mother's patently unsuitable choice of partner was not one of anger or even disappointment, rather he professed himself to be highly pleased with the situation, and in this way he avoided becoming aware of negative, conflicting feelings towards his mother. Greg's relationship with his mother was clearly a complex one and it was not unlikely that her new relationship was, in part, an unconscious reaction to her son's abandonment of her in favour of university. At the same time, it was probable that Greg harboured unconscious feelings of jealousy about his mother's new relationship and that his enthusiasm was also therefore a reaction against these feelings.

Leaving home to attend university is one of the bigger steps in the gradual processes of separation that culminate in independence and as such it is attended by a great deal of anxiety. In order to be able to engage fully in life at university, there has to be a commensurate disengagement with life at home, and that inevitably entails the experience of loss. As ever, to move forward, the past has to be left behind. A process of mourning has to be gone through and progress is eased by an awareness that what is left behind continues to exist and can be revisited, for some time at least. (This wish for the past to remain available is readily apparent in the complaints students make about their parents redecorating their rooms after they have left home.) From this perspective, it follows that significant changes in the structure of the family around the same time that attachments at home are being loosened and new ones at university are being formed are likely to be experienced as destabilising.

While problems of the sort described here are not the prerogative of any one type of family, these examples serve to highlight the importance of family structure in understanding unconscious processes in the individual. For this reason, among others, family therapy, with its explicit and central focus on the dynamics of the family, can be a most effective form of therapy. However, family therapy is not a realistic option for many students, either because they are geographically separated from their families while study-ing, or because either they or their family are unwilling to enter into therapy together. For many students, the prospect of rejoining their family in order to sort out their problems may be experienced as a backwards step and as such resisted. In a similar vein, parents may be reluctant to re-assume responsibility for children who have left home. For some students, group therapy, which promotes sharing of experiences, can provide an appropriate forum for exploring family issues.

Further reading

Gorrell Barnes, G. (1998) *Family Therapy in Changing Times*, London: Macmillan.
Laing, R. D. and Esterson, A. (1964) *Sanity, Madness and the Family*, London: Tavistock Publications.
Pincus, L. and Dare, C. (1978) *Secrets in the Family*, London: Faber and Faber.
Skynner, R. and Cleese, J. (1983) *Families and How to Survive Them*, London: Methuen.

5

Finding an Identity: the Tasks of Adolescence

For many students seeking counselling, problems in relationships are often the central presenting issue. There are a number of reasons why relationships occupy such a significant position in the lives of students including the obvious circumstance of finding themselves in a new social environment. Notwithstanding this important external change in their lives, the principal determinants of their heightened interest in relationships at this stage derive from *internal* forces of development that begin to take effect with the onset of puberty and continue to evolve through the various stages of adolescence. If we follow a commonly accepted view of adolescence as consisting of three overlapping, but nevertheless distinctive, stages then, generally speaking, most students who come to university more or less directly from school can be described as having completed the earlier stages of adolescence. By the end of their undergraduate studies, they will, in the main, have made substantial progress towards the end of the next and final stage of adolescent development. The relative success with which each stage is negotiated will critically influence the outcome of subsequent stages and difficulties encountered *en route* will, of course, become manifest in the types of problems that the individual may later experience.

The overarching developmental tasks of adolescence are interrelated and comprise of becoming independent of parents and of establishing a secure personal identity which will underpin subsequent intellectual and emotional development beyond the confines of school and family. This process, by which the individual evolves a sense of himself as an *independent* being, involves the familiar leitmotif of loss and is therefore, inevitably, painful. The corresponding struggle to determine a sense of individual identity, experienced acutely by some adolescents, is recognisable in the familiar 'identity crisis' of adolescence. As in previous stages of development, successful negotiation of this phase depends on a number of factors including the individual's own resources, a supportive family context and a conducive social environment. In Chapter 4 we observed how family dynamics can foster and encourage, or restrict and impede, individual development, in this chapter we will explore some of the problems students encounter in their attempts to forge relationships outside of the family. In order to understand the various relationship difficulties that may arise, an appreciation of the main developmental tasks of each stage of adolescence is necessary. These are outlined below along with the more common relationship problems that are likely to be encountered during each stage.

Three stages of adolescence

The construction of a personal identity can be conceived of in terms of a series of identifications. Thus, the personality of the individual evolves, in large part, through the assimilation of the characteristics of others *as apprehended by the individual*. This is not a random process in that the objects of identification are not arbitrarily chosen, however, their selection is often unconscious in origin. For example, it is unlikely that babies deliberately choose to take on the attributes of their parents, yet it is clear that, over the course of time, this is in effect what takes place and one can discern, even in very young children, characteristics of their parents. As children grow older, this process becomes more visible as, for example, when a little girl steps, literally, into her mother's shoes. The drive behind this process of identification stems initially from the infant's dependence, and his ambivalence in relation to his dependence. Thus, in concrete terms, if he could incorporate and, so to speak, fuse with his mother then he would never have to suffer deprivations and frustrations on account of her absences. In this sense, identification can be construed as a psychological mechanism of defence (see Chapter 3). Of course, as the child grows ol1der, love and admiration also prompt identification (and, more consciously, imitation) but even in this the more primitive wish to appropriate that which is loved and desired is evident. Fear can also be a powerful force underlying identification; for example, a child who has been bullied may, through a defensive process of 'identification with the aggressor', become a bully himself. In identifying with his abuser, the child attempts to distance himself from his powerless position as victim and, by appropriating the aggression of his abuser, gain a sense of power and control himself.

The child's original identifications are usually with his parents and, as his horizons expand, with other figures of importance and authority in his life, such as teachers. Identifications with peers, though evident, are less powerful and it is not until adolescence that this pattern changes significantly. Adolescence describes that period of development which is marked by the onset of puberty at one end and the emergence into adulthood at the other. Unlike earlier stages of development in the child's life, adolescence is not primarily a continuation, rather it is a period characterised by discontinuity. Most obviously, there is an undeniable and irreversible breach with the physicality of childhood. The body and physical characteristics of childhood are lost and an unfamiliar and oftentimes disturbing set of physical changes have to be assimilated in a relatively short period of time. The adolescent's rapid alienation from his childhood body is typically accompanied by a sharp distancing between himself and his parents and a concomitant move towards closer relations with his peers as he tries to make sense of and accommodate the intense anxiety and confusion evoked by this physical metamorphosis. The accompanying shift in identifications, away from parents and towards peers, helps pave the way for the eventual break with parental authority and the establishment of an independent mind and a sense of personal responsibility.

As noted above, the principal tasks that dominate adolescence can be usefully described and discussed in terms of three chronological stages. However, before delineating these stages, it should be borne in mind that adolescence is foremost a period characterised by upheaval, chaos and confusion, and that there is considerable fluidity and therefore movement between these stages. It is not unusual, therefore, to witness an efflorescence of activity typical of early adolescence in an individual approaching the end of adolescence.

Early adolescence

This early period of adolescence, which may span the years twelve to fifteen, sees the beginnings of withdrawal from parents. During these early stages, the adolescent's identifications are driven by 'narcissistic'[1] preoccupations and this is reflected in his choice of relationships. Friends are chosen on the basis of their capacity to match his abiding concerns *with himself* and are therefore usually of the same sex. Friendships are commonly based on a sense of recognition and discovery of aspects of the self in the other person. For example, teenagers who feel themselves to be 'misfits' may be drawn to others whom they perceive as 'outsiders', like themselves. Friends may also have qualities or attributes that the adolescent would ideally possess himself; or, alternatively, they may fill the emotional vacuum previously occupied by relationships with his parents. While such friendships are typically intense, they are essentially self-referential and lacking in depth and as such are often temporary. In keeping with the narcissism, or self-love, that characterises relationships during this stage, homosexual 'crushes' are common and the aim of sexual activity is more often experimental and directed towards self-discovery. Masturbation becomes important both as a means of discharging tension (that may or may not be sexual in origin) and as a vehicle for exploration of sexual attitudes and feelings.

Despite the adolescent's increasing emotional independence of his parents, infringements of parental authority are generally nonserious during this early period of adolescence. Typical, and from a parental point of view, irritating, adolescent behaviours at this time generally revolve around the adolescent's disregard for ordinary conventions and include, for example, refusing to keep themselves and their rooms orderly, failing to appear at regular mealtimes and so forth. The adolescent's self-absorption is thus mirrored in their parents' perception of them as inconsiderate and selfish. At this stage, a sense of identity is achieved through wholesale identification with the characteristics of the contemporary peer group. A premium is attached to physical appearance, clothes, choice of music, and so on. While this group identity provides a social supportive structure within which adolescents can experiment and learn about their new attributes, its prescriptive nature also functions to exclude those individuals who are unwilling or unable to adopt its rules. For some young people, an inability to identify at this stage may be the first indication of subsequent problems in identity formation. The following example demonstrates how one

---

[1] *Narcissus* was a youth in Greek mythology who fell in love with his own reflection. The term 'narcissism' derives from this myth and, in its broadest sense, refers to 'self-love'.

such individual was enabled to enter the early stages of adolescence with the help of a period of counselling.

Through her description of her early family life, Kelly conveyed an impression of a socially withdrawn family who not only failed to communicate with one another but who also subtly discouraged her demands for emotional contact with them. When she was eleven years old, her family moved to another town and she enrolled in a new school. Around the same time her periods started. She had not been prepared for the onset of puberty and, on top of all the other changes in her life, she felt emotionally overwhelmed by the upheavals in both the world outside her and in her internal world. Unused to sharing her feelings with others, Kelly withdrew further from her family and from her peers and immersed herself in her school work. She began to experience episodes of depression but said nothing about this. Although she made no friends at school her academic progress was good and she eventually left home to attend university in another town. However, her self-imposed social isolation had created in her an intense anxiety about her social acceptability and, despite an intense desire for friendships with her peers, she was too frightened to make any contact. During her second year Kelly became severely depressed and she was advised to defer her studies. She returned to live with her parents and her GP referred her for counselling. Although she found the experience of counselling extremely difficult, she thought that it was helping her and she persevered with it. Eventually she became friends with two girls who worked in the same store in which she had taken up temporary employment during her absence from university; the following year she felt well enough to resume her studies. Following her counsellor's advice, Kelly sought further help from the university counselling service. Kelly's androgynous and very youthful physical appearance suggested that her sexuality might be an area of confusion for her and this was confirmed when she stated that although she had had a lesbian relationship (with one of her friends from the store), she was not particularly attracted to women. She was similarly uncertain about her sexual feelings in relation to men. While her previous counselling had clearly helped her to overcome her initial terror about making contact with her peers, she recognised that she lagged a long way behind her peers in establishing relationships.

In this example, we can see how Kelly was helped, through the provision of a 'containing relationship' in her counselling, to move onto the stage of early adolescence. Once there, the relationships she formed were characteristic of that phase of development and were essentially narcissistic in type, their aim being to explore her own personal and sexual identity.

As discussed above, the formation of meaningful peer relationships plays a central role in the adolescent's growing sense of independence. The following example describes how one postgraduate student who had severe difficulties in establishing relationships beyond a superficial level, managed to circumvent her problems in this regard until she was faced with the prospect of having to leave university.

Ellen, a highly intelligent and shy young woman, was in the final year of her postgraduate studies when she began to suffer from panic attacks. Although she had always been a rather anxious individual, she could find no reason for these sudden and frightening outbreaks of anxiety now. Ellen had been a student at the same university for seven years; she had changed course as an undergraduate and this had entailed repeating her first year. After gaining a good undergraduate degree she had enrolled for a masters course which she had later converted into a doctorate. She lived in a university residence where she was a warden and she also worked in her department where she assisted in teaching undergraduates. She was on friendly terms with most of the staff in her department who occasionally invited her to join them for a drink in the university bars after work. She did not socialise much with the other postgraduate students in her department since they preferred to go to clubs and bars outside of the university; apart from a brief, and non-sexual, relationship with a young man on her course during her second year, she had had no other relationships of a 'romantic' sort. Although the members of her department were friendly to her, her relations with them did not amount to friendships in any substantial sense. However, despite her lack of deeper relationships, Ellen had not been unhappy. Her duties as a warden and assistant teacher, as well as her contact with her teachers and supervisors, provided her with some social contact and she did not worry overtly about finding a boyfriend or having girlfriends to confide in. In this way, by attaching herself to the institution rather than to an individual, Ellen had found a solution of sorts to the problem of relating to others. She had found a comfortable and protected niche for herself in the 'safe arms' of the university and it seemed likely, therefore, that the imminent loss of this protective 'relationship' underlay her panic attacks. Ellen's fears about leaving the sanctuary of the university were essentially fears about separation and, along with the lack of differentiated relationships in her life, suggested that she has not progressed beyond a very early stage in the process of separation and individuation (see Chapter 3) that lies at the heart of emotional development.

Middle adolescence

Middle adolescence, which typically begins around fifteen years and continues until seventeen or eighteen years, is the stage during which parental authority comes under serious threat. For many adolescents, their challenge to the accepted order is not especially dramatic in form and can usually be tolerated, if not understood or openly accepted, by their parents and society. For example, one of the more familiar areas of divergence between parents and adolescents is that of attitudes towards sex. Here, overt conflict is often avoided by a combination of the adolescent's secretiveness about their actual sexual activity and their parents' reluctance to know about it. For some other individuals, however, their assault on the status quo is a much stormier affair and demonstrates clearly their underlying struggle for independence. It is as though, in searching for their own ideas and values, these adolescents feels driven to challenge and attack the views of their parents, almost as if they have to divest themselves of any connection with them in order to make their own progress. In ridding himself of the potent influences and connections of his childhood, the adolescent creates a vacuum which, in part, accounts for his particular susceptibility to powerful ideologies which proffer omnipotent solutions with which he can identify. His attempts to master his internal emotional turmoil through his capacity for reason also resonate with, and therefore render him vulnerable to, the power of ideas. The severing of parental attachments leads the adolescent in search of new figures in whom he can emotionally invest; while relationships with peers absorb some of this energy, a continuing dependence on 'parental figures' may be discerned in the attraction that powerful charismatic leaders hold for some adolescents (and indeed, for many adults who may be 'stuck' at this level of development). The particular susceptibility of adolescents to cults, religious or otherwise, reflects some of the ambivalence inherent in the adolescent's struggle for independence.

At the same time, the heightened emotionality of adolescence fosters a ready attraction to emotionally charged issues which offer an opportunity for the discharge of feelings. Thus, emotive campaigns can be used (as well as served) by the adolescent as an outlet for the intense feelings they are experiencing. In their rejection of the power and authority invested in their parents, some adolescents take up common cause with the 'victims' of their parents' generation, for example, the concern expressed by many adolescents for the state of the environment and the (mis)treatment of animals can be seen to reflect this position. At an unconscious level, these concerns also represent an attempt to repair and make up for damage that has occurred in their internal world as a consequence of their battles for independence with their parents. The following example is illustrative of one young woman's efforts to establish her independence.

Maureen joined the Labour Party society at her university in her first week and, by the end of the term, had become secretary of the society. She was a vocal and active member, attending all of the meetings and most of the events supported by the society, in addition she spent many hours preparing and distributing leaflets, often at the expense of her studies. She had few friends on her course and her social life revolved around her political activities. A brief sexual relationship with the president of the society had ended abruptly when he dropped her for a new member of the society whom she described disparagingly as 'a political novice, an airhead'. She found it difficult to make friends with other women and felt uncomfortable with them. She was disparaging of their 'girly' interests and, as if to underscore her disinterest in her own femininity, she dressed shabbily and plainly paid scant attention to her appearance. Maureen had been the first member of her family to go to university. She was scathing about her father whom she depicted as a 'fascist', a man with entrenched opinions that he imposed on others, regardless of their views. While not close to her mother, her attitude to her was softer than towards her father and she painted a picture of a kindhearted but weak woman who agreed with her father to avoid trouble. As a teenager, she recalled arguing with her father constantly, mainly about his political opinions and his attitudes to women, including her mother, which she found patronising and insulting. At the same time, she was also able to remember earlier and very happy times with her father when he had used to take her fishing. It had been a relief when she had finally left home to go to university and she rarely returned, though she rang her mother every week.

As we can see, Maureen had been very fond of her father when she was a young child, however, it would seem that their positive relationship gave way during her teenage years to one of acrimony and intolerance, possibly as a consequence of her father's growing awareness of her as a young woman. While she had no wish to emulate her father whom she now despised, the model offered by her mother was hardly more attractive to her. Terrified of ending up like her parents, Maureen had consciously tried to distance herself from them; this was evident in her complete rejection of her father's views and, at a more subtle level, in her neglect of her own femininity. Despite her efforts, however, Maureen's relationships at university were depressingly similar in their dynamics to those she had had with her parents at home. Her attitude towards the other women at university among whom she might have found friends carried echoes of, and suggested an identification with, her father's denigratory views of women; it also reflected the more negative aspects of her ambivalent feelings towards her mother. Her lack of intimacy with other women students mirrored the relationship she had with her mother and was indicative of her anxieties about becoming more closely identified with her. Her brief affair with the president of the society was not untypical of her relationships with men and confirmed her view of men as lacking respect for women and only being interested in one thing, sex. Thus, the identity that Maureen had forged was heavily and adversely influenced by the more negative aspects of her relationships with her parents and, despite superficial appearances to the contrary, she was emotionally insecure and lacked confidence in herself.

The middle stage of adolescence is also the period during which narcissism begins to fail as a basis upon which satisfying relationships are built. The need for approval from peers gains importance and consideration of the needs of others becomes a significant factor. The decline in narcissistic relating is closely linked to another major developmental task of this period, namely, the working out of a stable sexual identity. Essentially, the process of detachment from the parents as the primary figures of love, which has as its first step the intense love affair with the self that is so characteristic of young adolescents, continues during this stage with the redirection of love on to others, usually of the *opposite* sex. Unresolved difficulties at this stage of development include the not uncommon preference shown by some female students for men considerably older than themselves, reflecting, in some instances, problems in giving up an unconscious attachment to their father. Promiscuous sexual behaviour, also not unusual at this age, despite its apparent proclamation of a maturing sexual identity may, in fact, be driven by unconscious conflicts arising out of unsatisfying attachments to the primary figure, usually the mother. Under these circumstances, the adolescent's attempts at using sexual relationships to circumvent dependency needs generally fail; the attendant misery then drives them to seek solace in further sexual liaisons and, when these inevitably fail, into depression. This cycle, propelled by unacknowledged dependence, is readily apparent in the following example.

Sally was in her third and final year at university when she came for counselling. She had been having 'boyfriend problems' and was feeling depressed and unable to concentrate on her studies. She had consulted her GP who had prescribed anti-depressant medication and advised her to attend the counselling service. Sally was the youngest of five children. Her parents ran their own business which appeared to take up all their time and energy leaving little over for the children. She recalled how she and her brothers and sisters took turns to do all the household chores because her parents had neither the time themselves nor the money to pay for additional help. She also remembered her mother as being constantly tired and irritable and she had learned early on not to bother her with her problems. Her relationships with her brothers and sisters were not close and there seemed to be a good deal of competition and resentment among the children for what limited parental resources there were. For example, Sally crossly described how one of her sisters had demanded and got money from their father for concert tickets when her mother had been complaining to her only the week before that she had insufficient money to renew their television licence. Although Sally had a reasonably paid part-time job, she spent most of her earnings on clothes and was consequently often short of money and worries about money were contributing to her present depressed state. The other major issue on her mind was her new boyfriend, whom she liked very much. She had known him for some time as a friend and they had recently started going out together; she was now worried that she would spoil things between them. She explained that all her previous relationships had been short-lived affairs and although she felt unable to control herself, she was aware of how destructive her behaviour had been in these relationships. She had got together with her new boyfriend at a party a few weeks earlier at which she had, as usual, drunk too much. He had helped her home and, at her invitation, stayed the night. They spent the rest of the weekend together and he returned to his flat on Monday promising to ring her during the week. On Thursday, when he had still not rung, she went out on her own to a club where she got drunk. She let a stranger pick her up and eventually went home with him to his flat. She returned to her room the following morning feeling angry and disgusted with herself to find a message that her 'boyfriend' had rung during the previous evening with an apology for not having rung sooner and a promise that he would try again later. When he rang she was off-hand and conveyed an indifference that she did not feel but she could not bring herself to confess her interest in seeing him again. Perhaps put off by her coolness, he did not press for a further meeting. The following weekend they came across each other in the student union bar where she again had too much to drink. As on the previous occasion he took her home and they spent the weekend together. She was now waiting for him to call her and was afraid that if he did not ring her soon, then she would be tempted to go out and pick someone up as she had done before. When it was suggested to her that she might call him, she was resolute that she could not do so and that on no account could she let him know that she was missing him.

In this case Sally's sexual behaviour can be understood in terms of an attempt to ward off any awareness in herself of a deep longing to be looked after. By getting drunk and becoming incapable of looking after herself, her dependence finds indirect expression and satisfaction through men who temporarily take on the role of looking after her, getting her home and so on. She is thus able to maintain her fantasy of being a grown-up woman who is wanted and needed rather than a child who needs to be looked after, by sexualising and projecting her desires so that it is the men who want and need her and not the other way round. Under no circumstances is she willing to expose her child-like needs, indeed she is intolerant of them in herself. The origins of her intense ambivalence are readily discernible in her unsatisfactory relationship with a mother whom she experiences as not only incapable of meeting her needs, but whom she imagines would be angry were she to express them. In order to assuage her needs, she resorts to alcohol which serves to drown her awareness of her dependence as well as indirectly stimulating caretaking behaviour in those around her. However, when she starts to become aware of that aspect of herself that is intensely dependent – as she did while waiting for her boyfriend to call her – this brings her into conflict with another facet of herself that is cruelly intolerant of such feelings. Her 'solution' to this conflict is usually to minimise the importance of the relationship, which can then be ended relatively painlessly. When she subsequently feels empty and lonely she seeks solace in alcohol and, if she gets sufficiently drunk, another sexual encounter.

The clarification of their sexual identity is a central and pressing issue for all adolescents and confusion and anxiety in this regard are common at this stage. In spite of more tolerant attitudes towards homosexuality, many young men and women still find it very difficult to acknowledge homosexual feelings in such a way that these can be thought about and explored in terms of their significance for their sexual identity. Thus, an intense fear of sexual feelings for someone of the same sex may precipitate in men, for example, an outbreak of determinedly masculine activity as if this might consolidate their male identity. The need to prove one's sexual identity, whether masculine or feminine, is also evident in the promiscuous behaviour of many adolescents and underlines the insecurities that attend this process. While it is not uncommon for students to report, and indeed to have experimented with, feelings of sexual attraction to others of both sexes, this is often a temporary phase and a predominant sexual orientation is, generally speaking, established during this stage. Although the eventual recognition and acceptance that one's primary sexual preferences are homosexual may come as a relief to individuals who have been struggling with painful uncertainties about themselves for a long time, this is by no means a uniform response and some adolescents are unable to come to terms with this outcome. Significant among their expressed concerns are the *imagined* reactions of their parents, in particular they fear incomprehension and non-acceptance. Some young people use the move away from home to university as an opportunity to 'come out' and explore their sexual identity without their parents' knowledge and in the company of their peers. Those individuals who are able to use this 'space' *both* to establish a clarification of their sexual identity *and* to consolidate their independence are more likely to be able to tell their parents about their sexuality and to be capable of facing their parents' possible anger and disappointment. Intense fear of parental disapproval and rejection more often derives from the adolescent's intense anxieties about himself and his sexuality than from an accurate prediction of parental responses. Nevertheless such fear prevents some students from being able to think at all about their sexuality and this inhibition is sometimes apparent in students who may become excessively preoccupied with their academic studies to the exclusion of any social life. And while others may manage to clarify their sexual identity they may not achieve the independence that would enable them to be open with their parents. Indeed, some families appear to function in a collusive manner in order to avoid any acknowledgment of a potentially unwelcome sexual identity within the family. The following example illustrates this latter configuration.

Dominic, a second year student, had known that he was gay from his early teens and he gave no indication of any emotional struggle within himself about his sexual identity. His contact with his parents during his childhood was limited by the fact that he had attended boarding schools since the age of five years. He also recalled that neither of his parents ever visited him while he was at school. His father, whom he described as a strict and distant man, held a prestigious position that entailed frequent postings abroad and his mother accompanied him on these. Dominic performed well at school, both academically and on the sports field, and he appeared to be socially well integrated with his peers. However, despite his apparent good adjustment, there were indications of underlying problems. For example, he suffered from periodic episodes of severe depression and he had, on one occasion, taken an overdose of sleeping tablets prescribed by his GP. In addition, he had been disciplined on a number of occasions at school for anti-social behaviour. Dominic was aware of how hard he had worked at school to win his parents', and especially his father's, approval and of how he had vacillated between feelings of anger and indifference at his parents' apparent lack of interest in him. When he was eighteen he began a lengthy homosexual relationship with a man ten years older than himself. He introduced his boyfriend to his family without making explicit the intimate nature of their relationship. His parents got on well with his new friend, particularly as he was familiar with Dominic's father's field of work, and in their subsequent meetings and telephone calls his parents always enquired about him. Interpreting their interest in his boyfriend as at last indicating an interest in *his* emotional world, Dominic felt closer to his parents. When Dominic broke up with his boyfriend a year later, his parents stopped enquiring about his 'friend' and his fantasy of parents who could be interested in his emotional life collapsed.

In this example, Dominic's parents' unwillingness to recognise his homosexuality was patently part of a much larger problem of which his parents' disinterest in him was one part. However, Dominic's ambivalence about letting his parents know about his feelings contributed to this family's emotional distance from one another. Thus, he was torn between a wish to be what he imagined his parents wanted, to gain their love and approval, and a desire to be accepted and loved for what he already was. Unable to express his rage at their indifference to his needs and feelings openly to his parents, he found an outlet in his destructive activity at school and in his depressions and suicidal impulses.

In the three examples described above – Maureen, Sally and Dominic – the central issue of adolescence, namely the struggle to become independent from parents, is clearly discernible. For many students, the friendships they form at university provide an important, and arguably vital, source of support in this endeavour and the need for approval from friends and acceptance within their peer group become paramount concerns. The importance of such relationships is evident in the observation that difficulties in establishing supportive friendships are a common undercurrent in a variety of other, apparently unrelated, problems. It is not unusual to find that students who spend most of their time on their studies, and effectively isolate themselves from their fellow students, report a range of problems including lack of concentration on studies, disturbed sleep, feelings of depression and so on. For such students, the attempt to escape from their problems in relating to other people by hiding in their work has failed. In keeping with their difficulty in recognising an inter-personal dimension to their problems, they often eschew psychological understanding and prefer explanations that offer emotionally neutral solutions. For example, one student who had clearly had problems in relating to others throughout his life, insisted that he was depressed because of a neurological chemical imbalance and that his substantial relationship difficulties were consequent upon this fact.

One area in which the struggle to establish and maintain satisfactory relationships typically becomes fraught is flat or house sharing. The following example illustrates the sorts of problems that commonly arise. In his second year at university, Bruce moved into a flat with three other students, two of whom, Surinder and Lenny, he had met in his halls of residence the previous year. The third student, Claire, was a good friend of Surinder's. From the outset it was clear that Lenny and Claire were attracted to one another and after a short while they began 'going out' together. While there was no doubt that Lenny and Claire spent more time with each other than with either Surinder or Bruce, they were sensitive about the problems of a couple sharing with other single people and were mindful not to seclude themselves or impose their relationship on the others. Nevertheless, Bruce grew increasingly irritated with every show of intimacy between them and eventually he felt that he had no option but to look for somewhere else to live. He had spoken about his disenchantment with their living arrangements to

Surinder but Surinder did not share his discontent and was not disturbed by Lenny and Claire's relationship. He was, however, becoming increasingly irritated with Bruce's complaints and he therefore suggested to him that he might find it helpful to talk the problem over with a counsellor. It emerged that Bruce was an only child. He described a lonely childhood and how he had longed for a brother or sister with whom to share things. His parents, who also worked together professionally, appeared to have had a close relationship from which Bruce had felt somewhat excluded. At school he had found it difficult to join in group activities and often had the feeling of being on the outside of whatever was going on. The friends he made tended to be other children like himself, also 'outsiders'. By contrast, his first year at university had been a wonderful experience. Living in student halls he had felt, for the first time, on the inside of things and at the heart of what was going on. On the basis of this, he had anticipated an even better year living in a shared flat. Clearly, he had not been prepared for the revitalisation of the old and painful feelings of exclusion that he had suffered throughout his childhood and the confrontation at close quarters with a couple whose intimate relations he could not ignore, and from which he was quite appropriately excluded, had overwhelmed him.

This example demonstrates the damaging effect that unresolved feelings, in this case jealousy, can have on the subsequent capacity of the individual to develop reasonable relationships with others. Another common source of relationship problems for students living together arises out of difficulties in expressing feelings such as anger to one another. Such difficulties are often understandable in terms of the individual's anxiety about the potentially damaging effects of disclosing their feelings upon their relationships; they may be frightened of being ignored, ostracised or laughed at on the one hand or, on the other, they may be afraid of hurting the other person. In either case, there is anxiety about the robustness of their relationship(s) and it is sometimes possible, as in the following example, to identify the origins of this concern in earlier relationships.

Diana had been feeling miserable for several weeks and eventually went to see a counsellor after bursting into tears during a tutorial. She was uncertain about why she felt so bad though, when asked about any changes in her life around the time she began to feel unhappy, she reported that a new flatmate had moved in with them then. Although Diana professed herself to be indifferent towards the new flatmate, her comments about her suggested a great deal of barely disguised animosity; in particular, Diana disliked her taste for unpleasant gossip. It seemed that Diana's other flatmate, also her best friend, was more sympathetic and did not share Diana's antipathy towards the newcomer. It seemed likely that her friend's more positive attitude had contributed to Diana's suppression of her own negative feelings. An enquiry about her family revealed that, although close to her mother, she rarely confided her problems in her because her mother would become worried and then Diana would feel bad for having upset her. She confirmed feeling irritated with her mother sometimes but added that her mother couldn't help it. In this case we can see how Diana's relationship with her mother is such that she does not feel that it is strong enough to help her with her problems, including those with her mother. Elements of this prototypical experience can be discerned in her current relationships where anxiety about the impact of her feelings inhibits her from expressing them and thereby potentially finding some resolution. As we can see, the new flatmate's apparent ease with exchanging possibly damaging information in the form of gossip, obviously disturbed Diana and may have precipitated anxiety in her about her own capacity to keep her negative feelings under control.

Late adolescence

This final stage, which begins around the age of eighteen and may last into the early twenties or even later, is a less turbulent one and, through processes of integration and consolidation, brings adolescence more or less to a close. The plasticity of early and middle adolescence recedes and individual character becomes fixed and sovereign. As a result, interests in work and the wider society become largely idiosyncratic; emotional preferences reflect the pre-eminence of the character of the individual; and sexual identity assumes its final form. At the same time as his externally directed interests take on an identifiable consistency, the 'late' adolescent's sense of himself becomes more stable and reliable; he 'knows' who he is, so to speak. This period, during which a permanent identity becomes established, can be a challenging one often involving 'identity crises'. Problems at this stage are commonly the outcome of failed or inadequate adaptations during earlier phases of development as illustrated in the following example.

Keith, a postgraduate student in his early twenties, had lost all motivation in his work on an experimental research programme and had become depressed. His present lack of interest in his work at this stage was somewhat surprising because the research team, of which he was part, was about to become involved in an exciting new project. Although his original reason for pursuing postgraduate studies had been a negative one, namely that he did not know what else to do after completing his undergraduate degree, he had begun to enjoy the work before he became depressed. The explanation that he gave for his current depression was that he had suffered from a bad bout of flu around the time that he first began to feel low. He did, however, recall that he had experienced a similar episode of depression as an undergraduate student for which he had been prescribed anti-depressant medication. At that time, he had become depressed following the end of a relationship with a young woman on his course. Despite his initial excitement about this woman, the relationship had been a brief one because he had lost interest in her and had ended the relationship. He had never had a lengthy relationship and, in fact, although his sexual experiences had all been with women, he had considered whether he might be homosexual since he found it difficult to sustain any sexual interest in his relationships with women. He did not, however, convey an active interest in sexual activity with other men and his curiosity in this direction seemed intellectual. When his counsellor observed that both episodes of depression had been *preceded* by a loss of interest on his part – on the first occasion in his girlfriend and on the second, in his work – Keith appeared indifferent to this idea and returned to his own explanation of events, namely that he had become depressed as a consequence of a viral illness. Subsequent attempts by the counsellor to think about any potential emotional meaning of his depressions met with similar disinterest and further 'rational' explanations from Keith; yet when the counsellor reflected his preference for more 'medical' accounts and suggested that he might therefore find an anti-depressant more helpful, he insisted that he wanted to understand why he became depressed.

The origins of this dynamic, wherein Keith appeared to want help in understanding himself but at the same time was rejecting of his counsellor's efforts in this direction, lay in his earlier relationships with his parents. Keith painted a picture of his mother as an emotionally distant, yet controlling woman with whom he had an apparently conflict-free relationship; his father appeared as a vague and uninfluential figure in his life. He could remember little about his childhood about which he seemed largely uninterested though one episode came to his mind; he had been caught playing 'doctors and nurses' with a neighbouring girl and they had not been allowed to play together after that. He had no idea as to why he had remembered this particular incident. Whether or not it was an accurate memory, Keith's portrayal of this childhood event, along with his description of his mother, suggested that he had internalised an experience of his mother as disapproving and punitive in relation to his early curiosity in sexual matters. (The important association between sexual curiosity in early childhood and the thirst for knowledge in later years will be explored in the next chapter.) Thus, to become excitedly interested risked possible censure *and* deprivation of the object that excited his interest. Keith had managed his anxiety about becoming excited mainly by erecting defences against its manifestation. When his defences failed, as they did when he started to become excited about his work, or when he met a girl who excited him, his powerful identification with a mother who could not allow such feelings became evident and he deprived himself of the source of his excitement. The loss of the exciting object precipitated his subsequent episodes of depression.

Returning to Keith's relationship with his counsellor, his reluctance to engage in an exploration about his emotional life can now be understood in terms of his defences against his fear of becoming excited and interested. In keeping with his identification with an emotionally distant and controlling mother, he is rejecting of the counsellor's attempts to engage him on an emotional level and he controls the field of discourse by refusing to take up any ideas other than his own. In this way he keeps the relationship with the counsellor within 'safe' limits, however, in doing so he stifles the counsellor's capacity to help him and an impasse is reached. This impediment to progress was plainly evident in Keith's arrested emotional development. He had reached the final stages of adolescence having failed to consolidate, let alone integrate, many of the important earlier stages of development. His sexual identity was ill defined; he had a poorly articulated sense of himself; and his attachments to, and investment in, the external world were severely limited.

For the majority of adolescents, their years in higher education offer an extended period of shelter from the full demands of adulthood, providing an opportunity for unresolved issues to be tackled again, hopefully with more success. This 'halfway house' also affords adolescents a relatively safe environment in which to test themselves and to learn about both their capabilities and their limitations. By the time they reach the end of their studies, most students are ready and eager to confront the challenges that lie ahead of them as adults. Some students, however, are less enthusiastic about the prospect of leaving university and taking up employment and they may avoid this next step in a number of ways such as failing examinations, thus necessitating a repeat year or, more creatively, by enrolling in postgraduate studies. For some, this respite may be enough to enable them to reach a stage where they feel more ready to leave, for others it may only represent a postponement of their ejection into an adult world that they still feel ill-equipped for, as in the example of Ellen described earlier.

As we have seen, the capacity to form and sustain meaningful relationships has its roots in early family relationships. It follows, therefore, that the individual's later attempts to form relationships during the various stages of adolescence will reflect his earlier efforts and will, to some extent, be limited by his earlier successes and failures. At the same time, however, both adolescence and the university experience afford the individual new possibilities and an opportunity to find fresh solutions to old problems; a second bite at the cherry, so to speak.

Further reading

Anderson, R. and Dartington, A. (eds) (1998) *Facing It Out: Clinical Perspectives on Adolescent Disturbance,* London: Duckworth.
Blos, P. (1962) *Adolescence,* New York: Macmillan.
Erikson, E. (1968) *Identity: Youth and Crisis,* New York: Norton.
Sayers, J. (1998) *Boy Crazy: Remembering Adolescence, Therapies and Dreams,* London: Routledge.
Van Heeswyk, P. (1997) *Analysing Adolescence,* London: Sheldon.

6

Learning and Study Problems

Of the many reasons why students choose to enter university, the desire for further education itself is not always paramount. Sometimes the decision to go to university is less an active choice and more a passive acquiescence, conscious or unconscious, with parental expectations; often it represents the fall-back option for individuals who have little idea what they want to do after leaving school. Even for those for whom university is a positive choice, the primary goal may not be further education itself; rather university may be seen as a way out of a painful family situation or as an opening into a wider social context. However, whatever the student's original motives for entering university, they may only remain there if they are able to engage in the primary overt task of the university, namely that of continuing their education. It is not surprising, therefore, that a significant proportion of students seeking help present with problems associated with the learning process. Before we examine some of the more common difficulties that students experience with their academic work over the course of their studies, it will be helpful to look in more detail at some of the processes ordinarily involved in learning. The emphasis on intellectual understanding in higher education has potential advantages and disadvantages for the counselling process which takes as its focus, feelings. We will consider briefly the difficulties that may arise as a result. Finally, some thoughts about subject choice will be discussed.

Learning and the 'epistemophilic instinct'

The old adage that you can take a horse to water but you cannot make it drink applies particularly well to the business of learning.

As every teacher knows, the task of educating a child is rendered both easier and more pleasurable when the child himself expresses a thirst for knowledge. But where does this thirst, or 'epistemophilic instinct', come from? There are a number of different views regarding the origins of the urge to learn. One perspective offers the view that the quest for knowledge evolves from the more 'primitive' biological instinct of hunger for food, that is to say, that the desire to learn is a developmentally more sophisticated version of the desire to incorporate, or take things into the self orally. This hierarchical view of development carries the implication that problems which are encountered at an earlier level, and are not adequately resolved there, may (re-) present themselves at later stages of development. Thus, we might not be surprised to learn from a student who complained of problems in settling down and concentrating on his work that his mother recalled that he had been a 'difficult' baby to feed. And when we discover further that he was a premature baby and that his mother had worried terribly about whether he would be able to take in enough food to thrive, we could say that the process of 'taking in', under these particular circumstances, had become suffused with anxiety. Thus, we might surmise that, for this student, anxiety about taking things in intellectually has historical roots in the nature of his early feeding relationship with his mother which was shaped by his premature birth and her anxiety about this. While this example is, of course, an oversimplification and many other factors contribute to and overlay early experiences, these first engagements with the external world take on a prototypical significance and influence subsequent development accordingly.

From another point of view, the desire for knowledge may be seen as derivative of an *innate* curiosity about the world and how things come about. In this view, epistemophilia is seen as emanating from an elemental desire for 'sexual' knowledge in the broadest sense. The child is driven by a desire to make sense of his own body and its functions and in the process gains the realisation that there is another sex, different from his own. Inexorably this leads to further lines of research and enquiry, often beyond that which can be satisfied by parents. For the young child the question: 'Where do babies come from?', is rarely a matter of prurient interest. Embarrassment does not yet inhibit such enquiries which spring from a genuine desire to know. That the child's curiosity begins locally, that is, with his own body and how he came to be, is hardly surprising. Of course, the sexual origins of the child's inquisitiveness become obscured in the subsequent elaboration and development of his innate curiosity. According to this view, we might expect that a child whose inquisitive behaviour is ignored or discouraged repeatedly, might later show a lack of interest in the world about him. Without adequate compensatory influences, such as may be provided by a teacher who values initiative over compliance, a child of this sort may experience problems in moving from school to university, where the corresponding shift towards an emphasis on self-motivated enquiry may prove to be beyond his abilities. In practice, it is difficult to disentangle these two perspectives on the origins of learning and together they offer a broader explanatory base.

Whatever the source of the drive for knowledge, differences among individuals in their appetite for, and attitude to, knowledge often become apparent at an early age. One commonly observes toddlers who are 'into everything' and need to be watched and restrained while others are shy and need to be encouraged to explore their environment. Less obvious, however, are the multifarious factors which act upon and influence each individual child's attitude to the acquisition of knowledge. While it is generally accepted nowadays that both physical and psychological development reflect the combined effects of genetic and environmental factors, it is rarely easy to determine their separate contributions. (This is an issue of great importance to educators and has been debated at great length in a number of areas including, notoriously, the issue of whether IQ – 'Intelligence Quotient' – is innate or acquired.) Nonetheless, in trying to understand the diverse problems that students experience in relation to their studies, it is often helpful to identify the various factors that have influenced their relationship to the process of learning. For example, one young man who complained of problems in writing essays reported no difficulties in understanding or collecting the background material for his essays, rather he was unable to gather the information together in a coherent form. A general inquiry about other issues in his life outside of university revealed that his aunt, to whom he was especially close, had cancer and was unlikely to survive. He added that his parents worried about him and had urged him not to think about his aunt and to concentrate on his university work. Further discussion suggested that this student's current problems with his work were a reflection of the emotional struggle he was having in trying to keep powerful feelings about his aunt from his mind. With his parents' advice in mind, he felt unable to collect together and think about his feelings which might have helped him to bear them more easily. Instead, like the material for his essays, they had remained as an incoherent and oppressive mass in his mind. This student was considerably helped by the provision of an opportunity to talk about his aunt. Another student came with a similar complaint, she was unable to present the data she had researched for her chemistry reports in a sensible and intelligent form. She described, with considerable frustration, how she knew what she wanted to say in her report, it was just that she was unable to express this adequately in written form. She did not recall having such problems before she came to university, however, she noted that at school she had chosen subjects which did not involve much writing because she had never enjoyed writing. Exploration of her dislike of writing suggested that this student might be dyslexic. This was confirmed by a subsequent assessment and the student was offered specialist tuition to help her with report writing. Although both these students presented study problems which were, on the surface, very similar, the factors underlying their respective difficulties were very different. The young man could not put things together in his mind because he feared being overwhelmed by intense feelings about the loss of his aunt were he to think about them, while the chemistry student could not bring structure to her written work because of a longstanding, though hitherto unrecognised, specific learning difficulty, in this case dyslexia.

In the following sections we will examine some of the more common problems that students encounter in the course of their studies. However, as will be obvious from the examples described above, similar outward appearances are not necessarily indicative of similar underlying processes and each problem has to be assessed in the particular context of the individual to whom the problem belongs. Assessment plays a central role in reaching a decision about what subsequent help will be most suitable for an individual student and is, therefore, an essential part of a counsellor's work with students. The assessment process, and its importance in determining appropriate levels of treatment and support, is explored in more detail in Chapter 8.

Loss of concentration

Many people can recall occasions when they have become so engrossed in a piece of work or study that they have not noticed the passage of time. Often they express surprise when they emerge from whatever they have been preoccupied with and realise how long they have been 'absent'. While total absorption of this sort is not, for most people, sustainable at an everyday level, the ability to focus one's attention and concentrate for lengthy periods without being distracted, is particularly important in academic study. In this context, the effects of anxiety on the individual's capacity for concentration are interesting. For example, while it might seem obvious that high levels of anxiety would interfere with a person's ability to concentrate, this is not inevitably so; some individuals with particularly low thresholds for anxiety manage by withdrawing into a circumscribed, and perforce more controllable, area of interest. This type of defence is not uncommon among students who suffer from severe forms of social anxiety; they may retreat into their academic work as an escape from the unmanageable anxiety they experience in social encounters. Again, a certain level of anxiety can be beneficial in concentrating the mind upon a particular activity; many students describe working better under the pressure of exam or essay deadlines. In the main, however, the capacity to concentrate is developed over time and flourishes under conditions where the child's interest and curiosity are sufficiently stimulated without being overwhelmed and are not constantly constrained or impeded by internal or external distractions. The business of maintaining this delicate balance falls initially to parents who help the young child to maintain a focus on the task in hand, for example, during feeding. Later teachers take on this auxiliary role, helping the child to keep his attention on a specific activity for a period of time. As most teachers will be able to testify, holding the attention of young children is not easy and requires a good deal of skill and ingenuity and even then is rarely sustainable for more than a short while. If the task in hand is too simple, or insufficiently challenging, then interest will be quickly lost; on the other hand, if it is too difficult, or overly demanding, then the child may become frustrated and turn away. Either way, concentration is lost. To complicate the situation further, there are usually a number of issues competing for the individual's attention at any one time and discipline is required in order to keep focussed on one particular area. This is especially so when the subject in hand demands a great deal of effort and it would be a relief to turn away from it and towards something more immediately rewarding. Discipline in this context refers to the individual's tolerance for frustration and, again, varies considerably. It is an important factor in concentration and underlies many of the difficulties in concentration experienced by students; for example, one student described how whenever he came to an especially difficult section in his economics textbook, his thoughts would drift off to his plans for the coming weekend, and he would find that although he had read the page, he could recall nothing of what he had just read.

Problems in concentrating on academic work are experienced by most students at some stage and individuals vary enormously in their reaction to such lapses in their ability to focus on their work. For some the experience is of a temporary setback; their expectation is that 'normal service' will be resumed shortly, and they do not become especially anxious. These students are able to tolerate the anxiety that accompanies the temporary loss of a necessary function and are, in general, capable of engaging in other, perhaps recreational, activities because they retain a belief that their capacity to work will be restored to them. Obviously, the more prolonged the incapacity, the more difficult it becomes to maintain such confidence, and robustness in this area is inestimably valuable for students who are often expected to be able to sustain high levels of concentration over inordinately lengthy periods of time. For other, less confident individuals, however, the first lapses in their ability to concentrate on their work generate a great deal of anxiety, bordering on panic. They may redouble their efforts to concentrate only to find themselves becoming more easily distracted. These students attempt to control the rising tide of anxiety within by seizing control of the external world into which is projected the source of their anxiety: they may, for example, become tormented by neighbours or flatmates whose noisy chatter, music, television, laughter – whatever – is felt to be the reason for their being unable to work. A temporary sense of relief may be gained from acting upon these perceived external sources of anxiety, however such respite is likely to be short-lived since the real source of anxiety remains untouched by such manoeuvres and, inevitably, once again assails the individual from within. Repeated failures to contain the anxiety provoked by internal threats to the capacity to work, in other words, the failure of more depressive level defences, may promote a shift towards a more primitive level of defence, and paranoid mechanisms may take over. If we continue with the example described above, the student's perception of his noisy neighbours as inconsiderate might then develop into the paranoid belief that his neighbours are maliciously disturbing him in order that he cannot work; the threat to his capacity to work is now well and truly located outside of himself. Of course this does not remove the threat, it does however relocate it in the external world and thereby affords the individual something outside of himself to blame. While relatively few students develop such fully blown paranoid ideas, many find the anxiety engendered by lapses in their ability to work hard to tolerate and seek external factors to which they might attribute their unease. Problems with concentration proliferate in the periods before exams and, unsurprisingly perhaps, this is also a time during which complaints about the inconsiderate behaviour of friends and flatmates abound. In addition, a significant number of students elect to return to the relative safety of the parental home to revise prior to their exams, again attesting to the increased sense of threat and consequent need for protection experienced by some students when the demands of academic work become intense.

The shift towards a more paranoid outlook is not, of course, the only response available to students who experience extreme anxiety as a consequence of losing their ability to concentrate on their work. The following example illustrates the response of one student whose intense anxiety eventually led to a breakdown in her capacity to function at university.

Helen had struggled through her first year exams with the help of her GP who, in response to her extreme anxiety, had prescribed a minor tranquiliser. As in the previous year, she began to experience problems in concentrating on her work in the month before her end of year examinations and, in a state of panic, she returned to her GP who again provided her with medication. He also suggested that she attend the student counselling service. Three weeks later, and one week before her exams, Helen telephoned the counselling service for an appointment. She turned up for her first appointment thirty minutes 'late' and a day early. She explained that she had lost her diary. She was given a second appointment card confirming her appointment the following morning. She failed to attend this appointment but turned up later on the next day in a dishevelled state. Her current state of distress was clear, as was her inability to bring herself along for her appointments at the prescribed times; it was decided therefore that an additional appointment would be created in order that she could be seen at the end of that day. Helen passed the twenty minutes until this appointment slumped in a chair in the waiting room to which she had been directed. For most of this session, she was listless and offered nothing of her own accord. From time to time she became slightly agitated but neither she or her counsellor were able to make much sense of these moments of heightened anxiety. Her counsellor judged that, for the time being, Helen was unable to engage in discussion to help herself, he was also concerned about her ability to look after herself following the session. Her address indicated that she lived in student halls and her counsellor was doubtful that she would have adequate support there. He therefore told Helen of his concerns about her and that he would like her to see her GP after the session. She said nothing in response to this but nodded when he asked if he might contact her GP to arrange an appointment. She nodded again when he asked if she would like him to accompany her to her GP's surgery. Later, her GP contacted her parents who eventually took her home.

It is plain from the outset that the student described in this example had a severely limited capacity to cope with anxiety. Her first year exams proved just about manageable with the help of medication and her GP's support. Unlike the first year exams, however, the second year exams counted towards her final assessment. These were more taxing and, not surprisingly, stimulated a great deal more anxiety. She was unable to tolerate this extra load and, as in the first year, she turned to her GP. His support and medication did not provide sufficient containment for her anxiety and, in an already fragmenting state, she contacted the counselling service. Her lost diary reflected her loss of her bearings internally and was readily apparent in the disorganisation that attended her visits to the counselling service. Her presentation both before and during the counselling session suggested a collapse of her defences and a regression into a state of dependency. That she had not sought counselling earlier, or contacted her parents about her difficulties, implied an ambivalence about seeking help which was only overcome when her situation became desperate. Her counsellor assessed that she had ceded her capacity to think for herself to him and he acted accordingly. Although Helen's acquiescence could possibly be understood as a further withdrawal into herself, her nodded agreement to his contacting her GP as well as her accompaniment of him to her GP's surgery suggested that he had made a reasonable judgement of her level of need at the time.

This case highlights the importance of assessment in determining the most appropriate course with a student. On the basis of his assessment of the student's current psychological state, the counsellor decided that what the student needed at this point was not counselling but active support. His decision to move his position from that of psychodynamic counsellor to one of active management in relation to the student involved a transgression of the usual boundaries between counsellor and student and, as such, compromised his future counselling relationship with the student. Such decisions, therefore, have to be considered carefully.

The example described above illustrates an extreme response to anxiety consequent upon the loss of a function, in this case, the ability to concentrate. For the majority of students lapses in their capacity to concentrate on their work are temporary. Nevertheless the attendant anxiety can be experienced as severely disabling at the time and, if it occurs when deadlines are pressing or exams are imminent, then the individual may panic. Under these circumstances, auxiliary support, in the form of concrete advice – for example, help in drawing up a revision schedule for exams – is often sufficient to restore a sense of agency. For these students, a subsequent period of counselling may be helpful in reflecting on how and why they become so disabled by anxiety and may enable them to develop strategies for coping with anxiety in the future. Some other students can manage to use the counselling process to help them get through a crisis and a brief series of counselling sessions may then be able to provide a much needed focus and structure for a student who has lost direction in his work and is in a state of panic.

Loss of concentration, especially if it is persistent and accompanied by loss of interest and motivation, may be indicative of an underlying depressive process. Under these circumstances, attention needs to be directed towards the student's depression and its causes and an assessment conducted in order to determine both the level of depression and the most appropriate course of help.

Loss of interest and motivation

Loss of interest and motivation in a subject of study is not an unusual occurrence among students and, as with loss of concentration, may be a temporary experience and may arise from a number of sources. For example, a student's disaffection with a particular course may reflect dissatisfaction with some aspect of their course, such as the quality of teaching on the course, which may be perceived as inadequate and unstimulating. However, the student may be apprehensive about expressing his discontent publicly and in a way which might engender effective change: he may fear that his views will not be taken seriously; or that he will be seen as a troublemaker; or even, that he is inventing excuses for his own indifferent academic performance. In this case, his loss of interest could be understood in terms of a defensive manoeuvre to avoid a potential conflict with authority in which he fears he will fare badly. For such students, exploration of their anxieties about voicing their concerns within their academic department with another member of the university such as a student counsellor, can often be helpful. This dynamic is familiar in families where the child may first approach his mother when there is an issue with which he is afraid to confront his father. In both scenarios, there are three parties, namely the child/student, mother/counsellor and father/university and in each case the child/student enlists the support of the mother/counsellor to help contain their fears of retaliation from the father/counsellor. Where the counsellor is unable to provide the necessary support, or the student is unable to make use of the help that is offered, the student may deal with the situation by denial and loss of interest or, if he is more aware of the underlying conflict and his anxiety in relation to it, by a conscious withdrawal. In either case, the cost to the student of not speaking out may be the loss of a potential area of study and knowledge.

There are, of course, many other possible reasons for students losing interest in their studies and, not uncommonly, a student's original reasons for choosing to study a particular subject can be illuminating in relation to their subsequent disaffection, particularly if this has been growing for some time. For example, some subject choices are made primarily in order to satisfy parental wishes, whether or not these are made explicitly. Meena, for example, went into medicine without a second thought, it had been what her parents wanted and expected of her and she had never considered anything else. At university, also her first experience of living apart from her family, she began to think for herself about her life and it was a painful realisation for her that she had very little interest in medicine. Parental influences in Meena's case were easily discernible, however, these are often interwoven in more complex ways as in the following example.

Jasper had been thrilled when he gained a place to study law in the same university as his father had attended. His only regret was that his father, who had been a successful lawyer until his death in a traffic accident when Jasper was nine years old, was not there to share his achievement. As his first year progressed, he found it increasingly difficult to keep up with his course work. While there was undoubtedly a lot of work to get through, he was finding it very hard going, and he often noticed that while he was reading his mind drifted off. When it was suggested to him that perhaps lack of interest lay behind his difficulty in focusing on his books, he protested heatedly that he had always wanted to study law and that he had his father's legal bent of mind. It gradually became clear that Jasper had never considered doing anything other than following in the footsteps of his father whom he clearly idealised and had never properly grieved for. His fantasy of *becoming* his father and of having the same mind as him had provided him with a means of avoiding the reality of his father's death and, therefore, of painful feelings of loss in relation to it. This fantasy had sustained him from the time of his father's death – when, interestingly, he remembered that he had not cried once – until he came to university when he could no longer escape the reality that his mind and its contents were not coterminous with his father's.

Loss of interest is also common when the subject chosen fails to match up to the student's expectations. For instance, students who are uncertain of what subjects they want to study at university, often make their choice on the basis of subjects they studied at A-level which they enjoyed or were good at. However, the change in style of teaching, usually towards a less structured format, and the greater intellectual demands of higher education may defeat students who are unprepared for such changes and who may then respond by turning away from their chosen subject. In contrast to these students who, lacking a clear sense of what they wish to study, choose conservatively, are those students who express a keen interest in a subject they have a limited experience, but great expectations, of and are then disillusioned when they discover it more fully at university. Psychology students, for example, are often sorely disappointed when they discover that the course they have enrolled on in order to explore 'how people tick' contains large elements of statistics, biology, animal behaviour and so on. While some prospective students investigate thoroughly the subjects they hope to study at university, many students opt for subjects on the basis of their fantasies about the subject. Subject choice is inevitably and quite properly influenced by emotional factors and unrealistic expectations of university courses are not at all unusual. Where feelings of frustration and disappointment are overwhelming, they may be expressed destructively through a wholesale angry rejection of the subject or through a defensive withdrawal of interest. For these students, it is as though an encounter with something other than exactly what they had in mind is intolerable and a threat to their integrity. The whole course of study becomes corrupted by their negative feelings and is then actively rejected or any interest in it withdrawn and an accommodation which would allow for the potential discovery or recovery of positive aspects in their new course becomes impossible. The majority of students, however, are able to make positive adjustments to the realities of their courses which may include changing to a subject more consonant with their interests.

As with loss of concentration, a marked decline in interest and motivation may also be a sign of depression as in the following example. Leo came for counselling at the advice of his tutor in whose class he had recently burst into tears. Leo reported that his tutor had been critical of a presentation he had given. On reflection, however, he conceded that his tutor's comments had been reasonable and, in fact, helpful and he did not really understand why he had become tearful. Thinking about his tutor's remarks about his work, Leo commented that he seemed to have lost all his interest in his studies at the end of the first term, some four months ago. When asked what else had been going on in his life at that time, he said that he had broken up with his girlfriend but also that he thought that he had got over it. Further discussion revealed that Leo had met this girlfriend two years earlier, around the time that his mother had died following a wholly unexpected heart attack. It seemed that his relationship with his girlfriend, a very supportive and sympathetic young woman, had buffered and shielded him from his intense grief about the death of his mother to whom he had been particularly close and that this protection was lost to him when he split up with his girlfriend. His depression could therefore be understood in terms of his unresolved grief about his mother's untimely death.

Work blocks

The experience of feeling blocked and unable to proceed with a piece of work is common among students and is generally transient. Provided that it does not arouse too much anxiety, the problem is often helped by the individual's taking a break from their work. In this respect, it is similar to the problem of loss of concentration described earlier. Subjectively, however, it differs from loss of concentration in that the student may report no difficulty in focusing on his work but rather that he is unable to make progress with it, as though he cannot think productively in relation to his work. Interest and motivation may also remain intact, but they too appear insufficient to promote useful activity. More often than not the origins of the blockage in his ability to think are inaccessible to the student and are frustratingly resistant to his attempts to disclose them. However, although work blocks may stimulate a great deal of worry and frustration, they are nevertheless an attempt, usually unconscious, on the part of the individual to defend himself against being overwhelmed by anxiety consequent upon proceeding with their work even though this is what is consciously desired.

Unsurprisingly, there are many possible underlying sources for work blocks and these can only be properly understood at the level of the individual. However it is not uncommon for unconscious fears related to failure or success to be found to be underpinning a paralysis in the capacity to work. The following example is illustrative of the potentially disabling effect of such unconscious conflicts.

Patricia had been an intelligent and popular girl at school and had been successful both academically and socially. When she was six years old her only sibling, a sister, was born. She recalled that her mother had been especially delighted to have another child at last. Her sister had been born prematurely and had required a great deal of attention in her early months and she recalled going to stay with an aunt for a few weeks after her sister's birth. Patricia remembered she and her father doing a lot of things together around this time and it seemed likely that her current close relationship with him stemmed from this period of her life. Her father had a strong interest in the theatre which her mother did not share and he often took Patricia, who shared his enthusiasm, with him instead. After leaving school, Patricia followed her theatrical interests and studied drama. She gained a first class degree and was awarded a grant for postgraduate study. It was during the final year of her doctoral study, as she was coming to the end of her thesis, that she experienced a severe block in her ability to work. She could find no adequate cause for this incapacity and, at her supervisor's advice, had eventually sought counselling help. Through discussion it emerged that her younger sister, who had recently taken her A-levels, had achieved mediocre results and would be unlikely to get into university. This had not been an altogether surprising outcome as her sister had always struggled academically. She reported that her sister had complained that their father had never showed any interest in her school work and that she had got no help with her school work from him. Patricia was largely unsympathetic and thought that her sister's complaint that her father favoured her was unfair and that in any case her sister had always had the lion's share of their mother's attention. As if to underline her point, she reported her sister's reaction when their father had offered to take Patricia to New York for the opening night of a major new production when her thesis was completed. Rather than being pleased for her, to her surprise, her sister had burst into tears and rushed out of the room. Patricia's rather harsh attitude in relation to her younger sister jarred with the rest of her presentation, which had been more open and thoughtful, and seemed to have a defensive quality as if she recognised some truth in her sister's accusations. When it was suggested to her that perhaps her sister had felt jealous of her special relationship with her father, she retorted: 'Well, she gets all mum's attention!' Patricia's response suggested a powerful unconscious emotional undercurrent in her relationship with her sister and it seemed not unlikely therefore that there might be a link between her sister's recent failure and her own block in successfully completing her work. It eventually became clear that Patricia had never really forgiven her mother for having her sister and that she had dealt with her anger and resentment about their growing intimacy by turning to her father with whom she developed a relationship which effectively excluded her mother and sister. In this fashion, not only did she find expression for her unconscious rage at being usurped by her sister but also she found compensation in her special relationship with her father. Although she dismissed her sister's accusations of favouritism, her guilt about monopolising her father in this way was evident in her defensiveness in response to her sister's feelings of jealousy about her relationship with their father. However, it was not until her sister failed her A-levels and openly blamed their father for neglecting her education in favour of her elder sister's that Patricia's defences began to falter and unconscious feelings of guilt began to press for attention. Obviously, completing her thesis and going off to New York with her father would have augmented her feelings of guilt in relation to her sister, making the work of repression even more difficult. Her work block could therefore be understood as an attempt at a solution to an unconscious conflict in which Patricia's desire for an intimacy with her father that excluded her sister, and probably her mother too, was pitted against her guilt in relation to her mother and sister.

As in the previous example, work blocks are often the visible tip of powerful unconscious conflicts which are highly resistant to examination. This is because the block is directed towards preempting any conscious awareness of the conflict and any attempt, therefore, in the direction of increasing awareness is strongly resisted and may lead to an intensification of the block. As a result, uncovering the conflicts underlying a work block can be a frustrating and difficult process and sometimes may be best approached indirectly. Thus, in the case described above, preliminary exploration of Patricia's family history and her current relationship with her sister was extremely helpful in thinking about the possible origins of her work block whereas direct discussion about it proved futile.

Performance anxiety and feelings of inadequacy

Fears related to performance during examinations as well as during presentations, seminars and tutorials are commonplace and beset most students at some stage of their university career. Although such fears stem from myriad sources, lack of confidence and poor self-esteem are typical themes. Not only is the student unable to make a realistic assessment of their own capabilities, anxiety about their perceived shortcomings may lead, via projection of negative feelings about themselves, to a distorted perception of the attitudes of others. Thus, they experience their fellow students and teachers to be unsympathetic and intolerant individuals who will judge them essentially as they have already judged themselves. The intensity of the student's anxieties about himself and the degree to which negative feelings are projected will determine the extent to which positive feedback can mitigate his anxieties. In the following example, the damaging effects of an inner world built up in a harsh and unsupportive emotional environment are plain to see.

Janine was an intelligent and diligent student who became paralysed by anxiety during the period preceding exams. This was in spite of the fact that she worked hard during the year and, from previous experience, knew that she had always been able to take her exams and achieve good marks. Nevertheless, in the weeks leading up to exams she would start to panic and would become convinced that she was stupid and would fail her forthcoming exams. Her work pattern would become erratic so that, too anxious to sleep, she would stay up all night revising and then spend the following day in a state of panic because she was exhausted and unable to motivate herself to resume her work. Janine's account of her relationship with her father seemed particularly relevant to her intense anxiety about her exam performance. He had taken a keen interest in her school work and used to help her most evenings with her homework. She recalled how when she got good marks for her school work she could hardly wait to go home and tell him. Although he was never effusive in his praise of her achievements she was sure that he was pleased with her; by the same token she was left in no doubt as to his disapproval of her when she fared less well. During her teens her father's attitude towards her changed, he mocked her academic ambitions and told her that she was a stupid girl and would end up a housewife like her mother. Her relationship with her mother had always been rather distant and she was terrified that she might become like her mother whom she saw as a rather inadequate and unfulfilled woman trapped in an unhappy marriage because she lacked the means to support herself independently. Although Janine grew to detest her father, it was clear that she continued to see him as the powerful figure in her family and that she viewed her mother with pity bordering on contempt. Against this background, Janine's severe performance anxiety could be understood principally in terms of her conflictual relationship with her father; guilt in relation to her mother was also a significant, though less obvious, factor. Thus, her strong desire to succeed academically, initially fuelled by her desire for her father's approval and fear of his disapproval, was severely compromised by his later disparagement of her capabilities. Janine was driven by a desire to please her powerful father; at the same time she was disabled in this aspiration by her identification with her father's deprecatory view of her. The lack of a compensatory relationship with her mother was also a significant factor. Her devaluation of her mother meant that she could not take refuge and find support in an identification with a mother whom she respected. Rather, she had formed an identification with a mother who was useless. That her father's attitude to her changed around the age she reached puberty, along with his scorn for her mother, suggested that his disenchantment with her was essentially misogynist and had probably been stimulated by his becoming aware of her sexuality.

In Janine's case, severe anxiety stimulated by examinations promoted extensive splitting and projection so that her external world took on more of the threatening aspects of her inner world. Just as she had been unable to establish a containing and supportive relationship with her mother which might have protected her from the more corrosive aspects of her relationship with her father, so she struggled to find any adequate reassurance in the external world against the terrors of her internal world. For Janine, exams were much more than an assessment of her academic attainments, they were a judgement of her worth as a person.

Provided it does not become the sole or principal determinant of self-worth, performance in exams can furnish the student with helpful feedback about themselves. For instance, confirmation, through positive results, of one's efforts is a satisfying experience and reinforces a sense of agency as well as potency, both of which are fundamental aspects of self-confidence. At the same time, the capacity to acknowledge one's failures, without becoming either totally identified with them or overwhelmed by them, and the ability to learn from them are also important. To put it another way, the ability to learn from experience is contingent upon the individual's capacity for *objective* critical self-appraisal and the ability to tolerate different points of view and this requires a degree of emotional resilience. Thus, a student who is able to manage his feelings of disappointment sufficiently to go and discuss a failed essay with his tutor is in a very different position from another student who feels too ashamed to approach his tutor. For the former student, the tutor is still predominantly a benign figure who can be turned to for help and whose alternative ideas can be tolerated and valued; for the latter, the tutor becomes imbued with the student's own negative self-view, his different opinions are felt as attacking and he is consequently experienced as unsympathetic. Difficulties in using criticism constructively lie at the heart of many students' problems in learning and are among the more intractable problems that students experience in relation to their work. In extreme cases, such students are exquisitely sensitive to criticism, which is invariably felt as a threat, and are easily upset by critical appraisals of their work. At the level of the unconscious, and in marked contrast to their conscious self-deprecation, these individuals are identified with an image of themselves as perfect and anything that threatens this conception of themselves has to be avoided at all costs. Their capacity to tolerate any challenge to their self-perception is severely limited and, developmentally speaking, we might say that they have a poorly developed capacity for functioning at the depressive level. The following example illustrates the deeply disabling effects such fears may have on a student's ability to learn.

Claudio had sought help early on in his first year at university at his tutor's suggestion. Much to the tutor's surprise, Claudio had burst into tears when his first essay had been returned to him in class with the comment, 'Next time, read the question.' Claudio later described how he had felt that his tutor considered him to be 'completely stupid' and that he had felt himself fill up with panic and had been afraid that he might cry in front of the other students in his class. When asked, he was able to recall that the tutor had made similar comments to several other students, however, this did not diminish at all his sense of being especially insulted or help him to put his own experience into perspective. Mixed feelings of fear and shame stopped him from attending classes given by this tutor and it was only when his tutor called him for, in Claudio's words, 'a special meeting', to discuss his non-attendance that he was eventually able to be consoled and rejoin his class. Claudio's family history was helpful in shedding light on his particular sensitivity to criticism. An only child, he had been brought up largely by his mother about whom he had very little to say. His father worked abroad for long periods at a time and his relationship with him was rather formal. It gradually became clear that his insouciant attitude in relation to his mother reflected his lack of separation from her and that his relationship with her was predicated on her narcissistic attachment to him; he was her perfect child. As a result, in his internal world, he did not exist for his mother in his own right, as an individual, rather his existence was inextricably bound up with hers. For Claudio, therefore, relationships did not consist of two separate minds which might, on account of their differences, sometimes come into conflict, rather his experience was of one coterminous mind. At an unconscious level he did not recognise or think about his mother as a separate person from himself and thus he had nothing to say about her. In this context, Claudio's extreme reaction to his tutor's remark becomes more comprehensible. The comment, 'Next time, read the question,' carried with it the implication that he had not understood the question in his tutor's mind and was therefore a clear indication that they did not share the same mind. In the depths of his unconscious, this represented a sudden assault on his relationship with his tutor and the tone of his relationship with his tutor moved from one extreme to another. Now he felt himself as banished from his tutor's mind as 'completely stupid' and was only reinstated when he felt that his tutor made a special effort to get him back.

While Claudio's is clearly an extreme example, the type of problem his case illustrates is not unusual. Narcissistic anxieties which concern the individual's fear of challenges to his self-esteem are ubiquitous and, under certain circumstances, may become problematic when they threaten to overwhelm the individual's ability to engage productively with the external world. For the majority of students who are approaching the latter stages of adolescence, when a firm sense of identity is not yet established, such anxieties are likely to be more common and are evident in the frequently observed, though usually transient, loss of confidence in academic abilities experienced by many students.

Intellectual understanding and counselling

One of the explicit aims of higher education is the expansion and development of intellectual abilities and, for many students, this coincides with a period of psychological development during which they finally begin to master the emotional upheaval triggered by puberty and the head becomes master of the heart, so to speak. It is also not uncommon at this stage to find that intellectual function becomes over-valued and that emotional experience is eschewed. It is as though, having attained control over the unruly feelings of earlier adolescence, the individual is loathe to re-establish contact with his emotions lest they re-assert their former dominance over him. His capacity to manage intense feelings is not yet securely established and he therefore tends to avoid emotional experiences that threaten to overwhelm his nascent sense of control. As we saw in our discussion of mechanisms of defence in Chapter 3, there are a variety of more or less mature defences that the individual may adopt to protect himself from becoming conscious of potentially painful feelings. It is not surprising, given the convergence of the pedagogic aims of the university and the developmental stage of the individual, that rationalisation and intellectualisation are particularly common psychological defences among students. In practice this means that they are more likely to turn to the external world for rational explanations of their behaviour, for example, the student who provides logical and reasonable explanations for his persistent lateness for appointments may be blocking consideration of possible unconscious reasons for his behaviour. Or, intellectual discussion of an issue may be used to distance the individual from potential unconscious determinants. For example, a first year overseas student who talks incessantly about the advantages for young people of foreign travel and study abroad may be trying to stave off an awareness of potentially overwhelming feelings of homesickness. At the same time, the ability to think about one's ideas and behaviour, including the capacity for intellectual and rational thought, is essential to the process of psychodynamic counselling. It would appear, therefore, that the emphasis on intellectual and rational thought at this stage in their development, both from without and from within, is a mixed blessing for students. On the one hand their developing intellectual capacities equip them better to explore their inner emotional world while on the other hand the same tools provide them with the very means to avoid any such adventure. In practice, both processes are usually in operation more or less at the same time and together they help to maintain an attitude of self enquiry that is emotionally manageable. Where the capacity to bear feelings is severely limited however, this balance may become upset as in the following example.

A student who had been raped by her boyfriend filled many

counselling sessions with well-reasoned, though emotionally dry, arguments to persuade herself that she had not been in any way responsible for what had happened to her. However, while she was able to recognise that she was not making much progress in this direction and that she continued to be plagued by feelings of guilt, the only way in which she could think about the matter was to search out further rational sops to her troubled conscience. The idea that she might turn her thoughts to what lay behind these unwelcome feelings as an alternative, and perhaps more productive, line of enquiry was unthinkable. After many more weeks in which she tried unsuccessfully to convince herself that she had no reasonable cause to feel guilty she eventually gave up and subsided into a rather hopeless and depressed state of mind. In this example, the student was aware of the futility of her intellectual strivings in ridding herself of feelings that felt alien to her, yet she was unable to make use of her capacity to think *about* these feelings because of the intense fear they evoked in her. As we discussed in Chapter 2, the capacity to tolerate and think about feelings develops out of the internalisation of early experiences in relationships with an adequately containing other, often the mother. In this case, the student's fear of what she might uncover in her internal world clearly exceeded her sense of her capacity to manage her discoveries. Thus, she could use her intellect to attempt to defend herself against her feelings but not in order to think about them.

Choice of subject

A myriad of factors, some more visible than others, influence the individual's choice of subject at university and may include: cultural background; family expectations, both explicit and implicit; peer group and the wider social environment; individual abilities and talents; self expectations and personal desires, which may not be the same, and so on. It follows, therefore, that each student's chosen course of study is an individual matter and can only be properly understood within the context of his particular circumstances. One of the more obvious decision points for students, the choice between arts and sciences, takes place long before they start at university and is often heavily influenced by parental wishes. Whichever choice is eventually made, however, it is generally the case that students whose personal inclination is towards 'soft' arts subjects are more likely to seek the help of a counsellor at university than those preferring the 'hard' sciences. We might surmise, therefore, that the sciences, and especially the 'hard' sciences, attract individuals whose interests lie predominantly in the external and rational world whereas arts students are more oriented towards internal reflection. For example, engineering students, on the whole, are less inclined to considering their problems in terms of their feelings and are more concerned to find practical advice and guidance with problems.

Another choice that is often made well in advance of the student starting university concerns the degree to which the chosen course of study is vocational. Some students enter university with a well-defined career path in mind such as medicine. For some of these students the certainty of knowing where they are going is reassuring and the clear structure of their course confirms for them the sense of being contained. Others, though, may feel increasingly stifled and hemmed in by the gradual shrinkage of their future options and may long to stray off the path laid out for them. Often these are students whose own reservations about their courses have been hidden, even from themselves, commonly to avoid conflicts with parents. Another group of students enter university with no clear idea at all of what they want to do after graduation. While they may not have an ultimate career in mind, some of these students nevertheless do have definite ideas about what subjects interest them and what course of study they want to pursue at university. Such individuals generally have a strong belief in themselves and are not unduly alarmed by uncertainty. In contrast to both these groups are those students who lack any firm sense of direction and choose their course of study at university on the basis of their A-level performance. These students sometimes evince a remarkable indifference in respect of their own interests and may even be disparaging about any interests they do hold. Their diffidence towards their own thoughts and feelings works against any creative function in relation to their own interests and their subject choice is consequently devoid of any serious emotional investment. Alternatively, previous experience may be eschewed completely and a capricious choice made upon a superficial impression of the subject, a strategy that may then may end in disillusionment. Some students use such disappointments constructively to inform a more satisfactory choice in the following year, either by transferring onto a different course, where this is possible, or by restarting on a different course. This implies a capacity to face up to mistakes and to learn from experiences which is not always available. For example, a first year student had elected to study astronomy in the wake of a resurgence of media interest in Roswell, the purported site of alien landings in New Mexico in 1947. However, he very quickly discovered that he had little interest in the academic study of astronomy and, as he was still in the first term of his course, he was able to arrange a transfer to another department. Having studied chemistry at A-level, he decided to change to chemistry. The chemistry departmental tutor agreed to his transfer but advised him to speak to some of the first year students in the department about the course before making his final decision. Despite his previous hasty judgement about astronomy, the student dismissed the tutor's cautionary advice as unnecessary on the basis that he had enjoyed chemistry at A-level and would therefore undoubtedly enjoy it at university. To his surprise, he found the chemistry course dull and not at all what he had expected and he eventually left university half way through the second term.

In the case described above, the student's choice of subject seemed to have been made impulsively, with little serious consideration given to how his various interests might be best met at university. The thoughtlessness apparent in his decision-making suggests a deficit in the reflective capacity that is ordinarily developed through the experience of a relationship in which thought precedes action, that is, one in which feelings can be contained and processed rather than immediately discharged. In the previous section, we touched on the use of the intellect as a defence against becoming aware of and thinking about feelings. In this section, we can see how conflictual feelings aroused by the need to think about one's own interests – in order to make a personally satisfying choice – may be avoided by acting rather than thinking.

Further reading

Socarides, W. and Kramer, S. (eds) (1996) *Work and Its Inhibitions: Psychoanalytic Essays*, Madison: International Universities Press.
Winnicott, D. W. (1971) *Playing and Reality*, New York: Basic Books.

7

BREAKDOWN, SELF-HARM AND SUICIDE

Karen was in her first year at university when she initially approached her university counselling service. She had been feeling increasingly anxious about her studies and had spoken to her academic tutor who had directed her to the counselling service. During her first session she spoke about how she had always been an anxious person and she added that she suffered from panic attacks when she felt especially pressured, for example, before exams. Despite her account of herself as a highly anxious individual, Karen did not convey any sense of the anxiety she complained of and her passive attitude throughout the session was very much at odds with her self-report. She offered her view that her problems stemmed from her childhood, about which she spoke vaguely, and said that she wanted therapy. In keeping with her general air of passivity, she appeared to conceive of therapy as something that would be done to her, as opposed to a process in which she might become actively engaged. Having accepted a further counselling session she cancelled it on the day leaving a message that she had to go away for a few days and would be in touch when she returned.

A year and a half elapsed before she reappeared. She described how she had gone travelling with a friend after her end of year exams, in which, despite her anxiety, she had achieved good results. While travelling in Ireland, however, she had become 'unwell'. She had begun to speak and act oddly and, alarmed by her strange behaviour, her companion had called out a doctor who had given her medication to stabilise her mood and had strongly recommended that she return home for futher treatment. Karen's description of her thoughts and feelings in the weeks prior to this suggested the onset of a psychotic process. Once home with her parents, she was seen by a psychiatrist who diagnosed her as having a schizophrenic illness and provision was made for her treatment within the local psychiatric services while she lived at home. However, feeling that her parents did not really want her living at home with them, and without notifying anyone, she left and returned to Ireland where, it seems, she suffered a severe 'mental breakdown'. She passed some weeks in hospital there until she was sufficiently well to travel and her parents came to take her home. The following year, which would have been her second year at university, sounded turbulent and included several moves into and out of her family home. By the time she returned to university to resume her studies she was again living with her parents. Within a week of the start of term however she had become extremely anxious again and was afraid that she might have another breakdown. She was more obviously anxious on this occasion and was offered on-going counselling and support which she accepted albeit with the accompanying remark that her parents were sceptical about the benefits of counselling or psychotherapy and that she was of a similar mind herself.

In fact Karen did not return to see her counsellor until the start of her final year, some twelve months later. She was again in a state of heightened anxiety and was terrified that she might fail her final year. This time she continued to attend counselling sessions on a more or less regular basis until she completed her studies and final examinations. From her account, the previous year had been another chaotic one and had included periods marked by severe paranoia when she had felt intensely persecuted by her tutor who had, in fact, been immensely supportive of her throughout her time at university. On the whole, however, she had felt that her academic department had been helpful and she was grateful for the continuous support they had provided for her. She had also come under the care of a psychiatrist whom she had liked at a hospital local to the university and this had provided her with another point of stability while she was studying.

Although she attended voluntarily, Karen remained suspicious of her counselling sessions which she used sometimes as a confessional and at other times to show off. She veered between manic states in which there was nothing she could not do and periods where the simplest tasks threw her into a state of panic. As her final examinations approached, she became increasingly anxious and a month before the exams she decided to withdraw. Her tutor, along with other members of her department, encouraged her to continue and she managed to take her final examinations. To her surprise and delight, and to the satisfaction of her tutors who were well aware of her academic abilities, she obtained an excellent degree class.

Two years later she wrote to her counsellor asking for help in finding a suitable therapist. Since leaving university she had had considerable problems in finding work that she liked and was currently unemployed. However, she had managed to find a shared flat in which she felt settled and she was hopeful of finding a job in the near future.

In Chapter 5 we explored the adolescent process and the main developmental tasks set in motion by the onset of puberty; we also looked at how these are commonly resolved in the context of the individual's relationships with others. While the majority of adolescents manage to negotiate this stage in their lives more or less successfully, the massive changes required in the turbulent passage from childhood into adulthood make adolescence a period of particular vulnerability. Emotional disturbance is to be expected and may be more or less severe, ranging from transient mood swings to more insistent psychological disorders requiring psychiatric treatment. The factors that contribute to psychological breakdown during adolescence are many and complex and their proper consideration is beyond the scope of this book. However, for the purposes of the present discussion it is important to keep in mind that the precursors of severe psychiatric illness during adolescence have often been determined many years earlier and are rarely attributable *solely* to the events of adolescence which may, nevertheless, provide the setting in which breakdown finally occurs. The hallmark of a serious psychological breakdown is the collapse of the individual's capacity for 'symbolic' thinking and his concomitant shift towards a more 'concrete' mode of thought. Symbolic thinking, or 'symbolism', refers to the vital process by which unconscious or repressed ideas, feelings and wishes find expression as, for example, in dreams; it provides the means by which the individual is able to reflect upon his inner world. Concrete thinking, by contrast, affords no such space for thought, and internal and external experience become confused as in the example described below in which a student 'hears' the 'voice' of his own unconscious in the whisperings of those around him. His capacity to think about his internal experience is severely compromised; instead he *reacts* to it, as though it were a concrete manifestation from without. The development of the capacity to symbolise proceeds from the earliest years and becomes progressively more sophisticated, underpinning our cultural life.

Where this capacity is not robustly established in early life, or where external demands become excessive, symbolism may give way to more primitive modes of thought and action. In this chapter, we will explore some of the more common manifestations of the failure to symbolise during adolescent breakdown.

Karen's story, described above, is a fictional account of the progress of a student, with a severe psychiatric illness, through university and is not untypical of a small but significant number of students with psychiatric disorders who are supported through university, with varying degrees of success. In this chapter we will examine the increased risk of psychological breakdown during adolescence and the role of the university and counselling services in supporting vulnerable students. Self-harming behaviours such as cutting, and attempted suicide are also much more prevalent during adolescence and we will discuss how one might be alert to early signs of such behaviours and what might constitute a reasonable response, including the involvement of psychiatric services. Finally, some consideration will be given to the potential opportunities for emotional development that the university environment can offer to students with serious psychiatric problems.

Psychological breakdown during adolescence

As already described in Chapter 5, adolescence is a period of massive upheaval during which the individual is engaged in a struggle for independence which is taking place on two fronts; on the one hand his body is undergoing a radical physical transformation that he has to somehow accommodate and, on the other, there is the pressing need to differentiate himself from his parents. This is a complex and often painful process involving a great deal of loss and, not surprisingly, is fraught with anxiety. The adolescent is torn between the onward developmental pressures that are accelerated by the arrival of puberty and strong regressive desires to retreat back into the comfortable familiarity of childhood. Progress towards the establishment of a secure sense of personal identity is rarely smooth and many adults recall periods of instability and fragility. Of course, this is not the adolescent's first essay in separating from his parents, rather it is another stage in a process of differentiation that has been ongoing throughout his life. The success, or otherwise, of his earlier efforts provides the psychological context from within which his latest strivings towards independence will be articulated. Where prior developmental failures are extensive, the outlook is not auspicious, although some adolescents are able to use the fresh opportunities afforded by the university setting to find different solutions. The following example illustrates one student's struggle to establish a sense of identity for himself.

Malcolm, a painfully shy young man, had been bullied throughout his years at boarding school. His parents had lived and worked abroad since he was a small boy and it seemed that he had not been able to impress upon them the depth of his misery. Although he did not complain about his parents' apparent neglect, it is probable that his sense of their indifference to his unhappiness fuelled his feelings of isolation and alienation at school. Having barely endured school, he described how he had felt as though he were floating on a cloud during his first three months at university. However, towards the middle of his first year he had begun to suffer from severe episodes of depression during which he would believe that his flatmates were whispering about him behind his back. His elation at escaping from his persecutors at school had faded and he had come down to earth only to find himself beset with intense feelings of insecurity and full of anxieties about his self-worth. He remembered that he had used to feel like this at school; only then he had attributed his misery to the spiteful behaviour of the other boys and he had used to comfort himself with the knowledge that everything would change when he left school. Lacking a secure sense of his own identity he had been acutely vulnerable to the comments of his peers. Now, however, there were no malevolent schoolboys to account for his unhappiness; and his desperate efforts to deal with his intolerable internal emotional situation, by splitting off and projecting the unwanted aspects of his inner world onto his flatmates, were now evident in his paranoid fears in relation to them. As before, his deep insecurity and fragile sense of identity repeatedly undermined his capacity to develop trust in relationships which would, ultimately, help him to establish a more stable sense of himself. Although at first sight it would appear that the experience of attending university had had a deleterious effect on Malcolm's psychological well-being, in the longer term it proved to be the start of his 'recovery'.

Malcolm had survived emotionally during his school years through extensive use of the defence mechanisms of splitting and projective identification. His projections had found concrete external expression in the bullying he suffered at school and this had enabled him to hold on to a stable psychological system in which everything 'bad' in his inner world could be re-located outside of himself, in the bullies. When he came to university, this system was no longer tenable and he entered a phase during which he suffered periodically from acute psychotic episodes. Gradually, with the support of a psychiatrist and an experienced counsellor, he was able to recognise his negative projections as his own and this marked the first step in his working through the very painful internal issues that he had managed to avoid throughout his childhood. While at university he continued to suffer from breakdowns in his psychological functioning, when he would become severely depressed and sometimes unable to get out of bed for days at a time, however, these became less frequent and less intense over time. Throughout his time at university, in addition to the support described above, he also received help from his academic department and this enabled him to obtain a reasonable degree. Perhaps more importantly for this young man, he gained a sense of identity and self-worth and was able to establish a small group of friends with whom he felt reasonably at ease.

Every year, there are a number of students like Malcolm and Karen who, with appropriate support, are able to make effective use of the sheltered setting that universities can offer to begin to work out fresh solutions to long standing emotional problems. The importance of the support available to both of the students in the examples described above cannot be stressed too highly and it is unlikely that either Malcolm or Karen would have been able to continue at university without the help that was available from the university teaching and counselling staff as well as from psychiatric services. In addition, both of these students were willing to acknowledge that they had problems and to accept some help, albeit reluctantly in Karen's case. Where students with potentially serious problems are either unwilling or unable to recognise that they need help, the outlook is bleak and a gross breakdown in their capacity to function adequately at university is not an uncommon outcome.

One of the principal factors that mitigates against a student's willingness to admit to having problems lies in the threat that this poses to their struggle for independence. Where this is poorly established, the individual experiences his need of others as a dangerous siren which threatens to drag him back into the dependent state from which he is so desperately trying to escape. Thus, paradoxically, it is often the student who is least equipped to manage on his own who is the last to present himself for help. Such students sometimes indicate their need for help in an indirect way, disowning and minimising their need and locating it in others. Thus, they may tell a counsellor that they have come because their tutor or friend or parent is worried about them; and while they may confess to a few problems with their work, they insist that they are perfectly capable of managing these themselves. Students who come in this way are acutely sensitive to remarks that carry any suggestion of their needing help; on the one hand help is precisely what they do need and it is important that this is acknowledged, on the other, to do so is likely to precipitate their flight. To fail to recognise their need for help openly is to confirm their fantasy of self-sufficiency as well as to foster their, possibly unconscious, sense of despair about their needs ever being understood and met. However, to speak to that part of them that might be aware of needing help risks an identification with the very figures, usually parental, from whom they are trying to distance themselves. The counsellor is caught on the horns of a very similar dilemma to that of the student: the student has come for help, no matter how indirectly expressed or overtly denied, and to fail to recognise this amounts to both counsellor and student colluding with the defensive and potentially destructive aspects of the student's unconscious mind; yet in acknowledging the student's implicit request for help, the counsellor risks overwhelming his defences against any such awareness causing the student either to augment his defences or else to flee. For the student the problem is essentially one of maintaining a safe emotional distance from the counsellor, for the counsellor the task lies in not coming too close but at the same time not going too far away either. Determining these parameters requires a great deal of sensitivity and therapeutic contact may easily be lost. Under circumstances such as these it can be more productive for the counsellor to make use of his countertransference identification with the student's dilemma and to address this. By describing the dilemma to the student, rather than trying to tackle it head-on, the counsellor is 'inviting' the student to think with him about the problem they share. This approach is likely to be experienced as less threatening and is more conducive to the formation of a working relationship between student and counsellor.

When students with serious mental health problems want and are willing to accept help, it is not unusual for several individuals to become involved in different aspects of their care. For example, over the course of her studies, Karen developed relationships of varying intensity with a number of professionals including several psychiatrists, at least two members of her academic department, her university counselling service and her GP. The relationships between these individuals, who become imbued with parental attributes by the student, take on an added significance because of their quasi-parental relationship to the student. It is therefore vital that an attitude of professional respect and tolerance is maintained among these various individuals. While this might seem an obvious point and hardly worth stating, relationships between the individuals who are concerned with supporting students with severe psychological problems are inevitably more susceptible to harmful distortions. This is because these students are more prone to use immature psychological defence mechanisms such as splitting and projection which tend to distort relationships. An example of this is the frequent playing off by a student of one member of their academic department against another, a dynamic that is commonly observed in families where a mother and father may be effectively divided by their child. Such students are likely to try and form an alliance with the counsellor, or whichever professional they are with, *against* another person with whom they are involved, as in the following example.

A student who suffered from severe bouts of depression had failed her exams and had had to apply for permission to resit them. She described her meeting with a senior member of her university department in terms that suggested that he had been extremely unsympathetic, to the point of cruelty, in his attitude towards her. The student was plainly distressed and her counsellor was concerned about the apparent mistreatment she had received. At the same time, the student's certainty and challenging manner made the counsellor draw back from a hasty conclusion. As the student described the interview with her tutor in more detail, it became clear that she had gone into the meeting feeling worthless and full of shame and that, in fact, her tutor's remarks had been considerate. However he had become identified with her projected negative feelings about herself. As a consequence, she had experienced her tutor's kind comments as though he was mocking her and she had felt that his helpful suggestions were meant to make her feel small and useless. In complaining about her tutor to her counsellor, the student was seeking the counsellor's support against the tutor who was now identified with unwanted aspects of herself. To put it another way, the counsellor was being 'invited' to collude with the student's unconscious defensive system in which the tutor was being used as a repository for the student's bad feelings about herself. While it could have been, of course, possible that the student's tutor had been as she described, it was vital for the counsellor to be able to suspend his judgement sufficiently in order to listen to the potential unconscious elements of the student's communication. Where contact between the various individuals concerned with a student is limited, the scope for splitting and projection becomes wide and confusions and misunderstandings can proliferate. A good measure of caution is therefore needed when dealing with students for whom defensive measures of this sort form a large part of their psychological armoury.

It will be clear from the examples described above that the role of the university counselling service in helping students with severe psychological problems is mostly a supportive one and that medical, usually psychiatric, care is also necessary. (Some students with serious problems can benefit significantly from intensive long term psychotherapy, though provision for this is generally scarce both within university counselling services and in the NHS.) This is not to decry the value of such support, which can be crucial to further development, but rather to highlight the limitations of what can be realistically achieved within the university setting. Universities can provide an environment that, for *some* psychologically vulnerable individuals, offers sufficient challenge and support to enable them to resume their emotional development, for example, in Malcolm's case. For others, however, the demands of independent study and the social pressures of university life prove overwhelming.

As already discussed, temporary breakdowns in psychological functioning during adolescence are not unusual and, with reasonable support, recovery is generally good. However, when problems persist and become entrenched, a psychiatric referral may be felt to be necessary and this has to be discussed with the student. The issue for the counsellor, or other concerned professional, is *when* to broach this issue. If the option of a psychiatric consultation is raised too soon, the student might become alarmed and take flight; on the other hand, if the matter is delayed too long, there is a risk that the problem may become more serious. The issue of when a student is most likely to be open to thinking about and discussing seeing a psychiatrist is a matter for the counsellor's clinical judgement and will depend on the relationship between them. There are, however, some signs that can be helpful in determining when such an intervention might be considered. These can be roughly grouped into three categories: the first covers university work and includes, for example, attendance at classes and performance in assessed work. Failure to attend lectures and tutorials for an extended period without warning or explanation is often an early indication that a student is experiencing difficulties. An unexpected deterioration in the standard of their academic work is another common sign. A sudden loss of interest in their studies, which may be accompanied by zealous preoccupations elsewhere, may also be indicative of serious psychological difficulties. Problems with studies are not necessarily apparent to the counsellor and may not be mentioned by the student because they feel ashamed or perhaps do not even consider them to be relevant. Part of the counsellor's task in assessing the severity of a student's problem might, therefore, include some discussion about their academic work. A second group of signs that may point to a significant disturbance in a student's psychological state relate to his level of social functioning. He may have withdrawn socially and may have stopped seeing friends. He may describe feelings of mistrust and irritation in relation to others and prefer to be alone; or that he seems short tempered lately and seems to easily get into arguments with people. He might report that friends and family have complained that they 'don't know what's got into him' and that his behaviour appears unreasonable. Where a student himself recognises a worsening in his social relations, the outlook is generally more favourable. A third area in which psychological problems may become apparent concerns what might be loosely termed personal care and habits. These include matters of personal hygiene and dress; a noticeable decline in these may be cause for serious concern. Similarly, obvious signs of weight loss or lack of sleep, as well as significant changes in either sleeping or eating habits, might be indicative of underlying psychological problems. Again, while the consumption of excessive amounts of alcohol or drugs is, to some extent, a 'normal' part of student behaviour, dramatic increases in the use of either may indicate a worrying deterioration in a student's capacity to cope. None of the changes described above is necessarily indicative of a serious decline in a student's psychological well-being, however their occurrence should alert those concerned with the student's welfare to such a possibility and a full assessment is advisable. If a student is unwilling to consider a psychiatric consultation, the counsellor's options may be fairly limited since most university counselling services have a policy of confidentiality. The aim of this policy is to protect students from enquiries from university staff, parents and other parties with a potential interest in them. While it can be enormously frustrating and painful for teaching staff, family and friends to be refused information about a student, many students, often those in most need of help, would not attend counselling services without this protection. Unless a student presents a serious risk to his own life or to the lives of others, the counsellor is generally unable to tak any further action on their behalf other than to continue, or discor tinue, working with them. Confidentiality policies usually refer to the counselling service rather than to particular counsellors and the counsellor is therefore able to obtain help in dealing with difficult issues of this nature through discussion with colleagues.

Suicide

While the academic and social demands of university may be experienced variously, sometimes as challenging and, at other times, as oppressive, they are rarely the primary significant cause for a student's committing or attempting suicide. Undoubtedly the risk of suicide among students increases before the exam period; there is also an upsurge around the Christmas period when social activity is at its height in the university as elsewhere. However, the majority of students who attempt suicide have serious psychological problems that pre-date their entry to university. This is not to minimise the pressures that do attend university life, nor to absolve the universities of their welfare responsibilities in relation to their students, but rather to emphasise the serious nature of the problems that beset students who attempt suicide and the implications of this for the help and support that they might need in order to continue their studies. It is important to recognise the complexity of factors involved in an attempted suicide and the need for appropriate professional help, especially in the enormously difficult task of differentiating between those attempts where the unconscious wish is for death and those where it has another meaning, for example, an attack on an abandoning or rejecting object. The assessment of future risk is also a difficult and uncertain matter and an expert professional opinion is advisable.

That death and fantasies of suicide figure significantly among the preoccupations of adolescents, and therefore of students, is amply evidenced in their popular culture. Given the essentially existential nature of the developmental task confronting the adolescent, an absorption with issues of life and death is not unexpected. At the same time, the intensity of the emotional experiences that occur during adolescence is not always matched by an adequate development in the adolescent's capacity to manage his feelings; hence the wild outbursts that so unsettle parents and often mystify adolescents themselves. A certain amount of poorly controlled, and even uncontrolled, destructive behaviour in which death may be courted and then defied is not therefore unusual and reflects the adolescent's efforts to come to terms with his own existence and to establish his own personal identity. The desire for mastery of his feelings also plays an important part in the sometimes frightening challenges that adolescents take up. However, for some individuals who are unable to negotiate a viable solution to these issues, the idea of death can become a compelling alternative to the insoluble and painful problems of life.

In a sense, attempted suicide during adolescence can also be viewed as a form of psychological breakdown, in that it is indicative of a failure to negotiate the ordinary developmental hurdles of adolescence. It also points to a collapse in the capacity for symbolic functioning, as the dominant means of expressing and working through unconscious conflicts, and a return to primitive and concrete modes where action takes precedence over thought. Typically the suicidal student is wrestling, unsuccessfully, with conflicts whose resolution play an integral part in growing up. The central concerns of separating from his family of origin and forging an identity of his own become more pressing with the shift from school to university and earlier difficulties in these areas become more visible under the added pressures of university life.

Every year a significant number of students make an attempt to end their own lives and every year a small number succeed. In spite of the relatively high incidence of attempted suicide among students, the surprise and disbelief that commonly follows each event reflects the immense difficulty that many people, including close associates such as family, friends and teachers, have in understanding and accepting the nature and intensity of feelings that can end in suicide. While a variety of complex personal reasons are undoubtedly involved in each case, an unwillingness to confront the powerful feelings that are inevitably stirred up in all of us by suicidal ideas and behaviour in other people, especially those we know, contributes to this apparent naivety in the face of suicide. Suicide, with its explicit repudiation of life and the thinking and feeling that goes with living, tends to provoke an immediate counter-response in others that embraces life and extols its sensory values. It is as though the destructive feelings implied by talk of suicide are experienced literally by the listener as a concrete attack on life and cannot be contained and considered but must at all costs be countered. A defence is therefore mounted against the incursion of the suicidal individual's experience. Many common responses to an expressed idea of suicide are an implicit rejection of the emotional experience of the suicidal individual and, as such, may increase his sense of alienation. For example, a not untypical remark such as, '. . . but you have so much to live for', vividly captures the gulf in understanding between the suicidal person and his audience and demonstrates the latter's failure to appreciate the emptiness that may underlie a suicidal wish. Likewise, comments that minimise the individual's suffering such as, '. . . things are not that bad', serve mainly to preserve the listener's own emotional experience and beliefs and to protect him from any real contact with the inner desolation and despair of the suicidal person. To identify, even partially, with the emotional experience of the suicidal individual is to enter a world in which destructive feelings vitiate against hope and, for most people, this becomes, eventually, unbearable. The recovery of hope, or to put it another way, the desire to live, is inevitably a huge struggle because it entails giving up the powerful sense of agency that being able to end one's life confers, and re-establishing contact with an internal world in which feelings of helplessness, despair, rage and self-loathing may predominate. As a result, this shift is rarely made easily or smoothly and is always painful.

For the counsellor, or others, concerned with a student who may be at risk from suicide, assessing the level of risk is a vital and often difficult endeavour and, where possible, a professional opinion should be sought. However, one of the more obvious elements in determining the likelihood of an actual suicide attempt, namely talking openly to the student about it, is commonly avoided. Part of this reluctance stems from a fear that to talk about suicide is more likely to make it happen and it is not unusual for academic staff, when expressing their concerns about a student to a counsellor, to reassure the counsellor that they did not mention 'suicide' to the student. The implicit notion that suicidal feelings and behaviour can be somehow controlled by denying they exist is clearly irrational and is probably an unconscious counter-reaction to feelings of helplessness that might otherwise assail the tutor confronted with a student who wishes to take his own life. An unwillingness to talk to a student about his thoughts and feelings about killing himself may also reflect a fear of becoming caught up in the student's problems; it may also reflect an appropriate awareness on the part of the tutor or other concerned individual, of his lack of training in this area. The anxiety that, by engaging with the student emotionally at this point, one will incur further responsibility for him is a realistic one and, at an unconscious level, may be a response to the enormous unfulfilled needs implicit in the student's destructiveness. These anxieties notwithstanding, it is rarely helpful to avoid mentioning suicide to a student about whom there is a serious concern and talking about it to the student remains an important element in assessing the level of risk of suicide.

Aside from asking the student directly about their intentions, there are various other types of information that can be helpful in assessing the likelihood of suicide. For example, a student who has been severely depressed for some time and who expresses an absolute hopelessness about the future is more at risk than a student who talks about his plans for the weekend. Likewise, a student who conveys a deep sense of indifference about his future and his relationships may also be more at risk than someone who voices concern about what his family will think and feel. These are, of course, only general observations and some individuals who have made elaborate holiday plans or who worry openly about their family's reaction do nevertheless go on to kill themselves. Suicidal feelings may form part of an emotional state that is highly charged and confused and therefore unstable and unpredictable. For example, one student took a serious overdose some weeks after the unexpected ending after five years of her relationship with her boyfriend. Her emotional state in the weeks after he left her had been extremely volatile and she had swung wildly between agitated states full of unbounded rage and angry tears and, at other times, periods during which her moods were characterised by lethargy and listlessness when everything in her life seemed pointless. She veered between hating her boyfriend and hating herself and her fury was redirected accordingly; sometimes she wished he was dead, sometimes she wished this fate upon herself, for much of the time she slumped into a state in which nothing seemed to interest her or matter to her. For this student, who had sidestepped the process of becoming independent of her family during her adolescence by substituting her boyfriend for her parents, the sudden and unexpected loss of the person to whom she had transferred her dependence had been catastrophic. Her rage and desolation were like that of an abandoned child and, like a child, she had not yet developed the capacity to manage her feelings on her own. Her overdose, taken after a phone call to her ex-boyfriend during which he had refused her request to meet up to discuss their relationship, was an outward manifestation of her inability to contain her feelings, in this case, of destructive rage.

The confusion of feelings that attend suicidal impulses can be misleading. A sudden change in mood, especially where there is a notable increase in excitement and level of activity, may be due to the satisfaction and excitement engendered by a sense of control over one's life, albeit the ending of it, and may sometimes be confused by those concerned with a suicidal person as indicative of an improvement in mood when it may, in fact, herald an imminent suicide attempt. It can often be helpful, in circumstances such as these, to discuss the situation with a colleague. The involvement of a third party can foster a space for *thinking* which is often pushed aside in favour of action under the pressure of suicide threats or gestures.

Self-harming behaviour

While it is plain that there is a relationship between self-harming behaviour and suicide, it is not a straightforward one. Not all, or even most, self-injurious behaviours are suicidal in intent. At the same time, a large number of those who commit suicide have a history of self-harming behaviour. Self-harming behaviours usually refer to direct visible acts of violence against the self such as cutting, scratching or burning the skin, hitting or punching oneself, pulling out hair and so on. In a broader sense, however, they also may include behaviours whose destructive action is less immediately obvious such as anorexia/bulimia, the abuse of alcohol or drugs, gambling or stealing, and so forth. The 'choice' of self-harming behaviour or behaviours will depend on various factors, principally the particular psychological significance of that behaviour for the individual. For example, some anorexics completely avoid alcohol because of its high calorific content while others use it to literally drown feelings of hunger; some individuals who pull out so much hair from their head that they cannot go out without a hat might nevertheless find the idea of lacerating their skin with a razor blade abhorrent. Whatever the self-injurious behaviour, they generally share the common overt purpose for the individual of relieving levels of tension that would otherwise become unbearable. While the person typically feels bad some time afterwards, when feelings of guilt, shame and self-loathing may be pronounced, *at the time* the predominant experience is of a release from anxiety and may involve feelings of euphoria and a sense of calm. Control is often a central theme in self-harming behaviour wherein the individual gains a sense, albeit temporary and ultimately self-defeating, of being in control over what happens to him: thus, by attacking himself he unconsciously aims to bring about a reversal in the dynamics of his internal world so that he is no longer helpless and powerless. The following example illustrates the fleeting and insubstantial nature of relief obtained in this way as well as the self-damaging spiral that ensues when self-injurious behaviours become a routine part of an individual's system of defences.

Despite the hot sunshine, Lauren came for her first counselling session in a long-sleeved sweatshirt and even though she was sweating profusely, she did not roll up her sleeves. She shifted about uncomfortably in her chair, carefully avoiding eye contact with the counsellor. Her distress was palpable, however, she seemed unable to focus her thoughts and say why she had come. Following a comment about her obvious unease, she became red-faced and slightly more agitated and, tugging her sleeves down, blurted out that she cut her arms. Gradually it emerged that Lauren had begun cutting her arms several years previously following a move to a new school. This had been the latest in a long line of changes in school and was occasioned by her father's work which took the family all over Europe and the Middle East. This particular move had interrupted her relationship with a boy whom she had especially liked and she had pleaded with her parents to let her stay on at the school. As it happened she had an aunt, living in the same town as the school, who had expressed her willingness for Lauren to live with her while she continued her studies but her parents would not consider this alternative and the family duly moved. Following this Lauren became sullen and withdrawn and had problems settling into her new school. Her school work deteriorated and she had frequent rows with her parents after which she would go to her room and cut her arms. She described watching the blood form into lines on her arm and how this made her feel 'lighter' and 'peaceful' and as if all the rage and fury in her was draining away; at that moment she would feel exultant, as if nothing could touch her. Later these feelings would seep away and she would be left with a deep sense of emptiness and self-hatred. In coming to university, Lauren had believed that her life would change dramatically and that, without her parents to tell her what she could and could not do, she would feel free and happy. On the contrary, she had been lonely and depressed for much of her first year and had found it hard to make friends with the other students who seemed, to her, to have all the qualities she lacked herself. Hating herself for her insufficiencies, she began to cut her arms again.

There are a number of different levels at which Lauren's self-injurious behaviour can be understood. Consciously, it served to relieve her of an unbearable level of tension. At a less conscious level her cutting might have functioned as a displacement activity for intense feelings of rage consequent upon her sense of helplessness about herself – for example, she assumed that the other students were simply born with the attributes she so admired in them, and that there was, therefore, no hope for her; at a deeper level, involving processes of splitting and projective identification, it might have served as a means of cutting off from and controlling her capacity to feel pain. However it is understood, Lauren's self-harming behaviour had become a means of dealing with emotional conflict, probably to do with intensely ambivalent feelings of dependence; cutting her arms afforded her a temporary period of respite which, when it wore off, was replaced by an intensification of her negative feelings about herself.

Self-harming behaviour like Lauren's is, at an emotional level, directed against the self and is driven primarily by feelings such as shame, lack of self-worth and so on. These same feelings contribute to the often hidden nature of the self-harm in these individuals. This type of action needs to be distinguished from self-harm whose emotional object is *not* the self, for example, as in 'attention seeking' behaviour. This form of self-harm is typically more public and has the underlying aim of controlling and manipulating the other. Such individuals often place enormous emotional demands on their friends, as in the following example. Shona, the room-mate of one such student, was plagued with conflicting feelings of guilt and resentment and she eventually confided in a tutor. Unlike her room-mate, Shona had many friends with whom she frequently went out. On returning one evening, she had found her room-mate cutting her arms. Shocked and upset, Shona spent most of the night talking with her and, after a while, her room-mate agreed to tell her when she felt bad and like cutting herself. On these occasions, Shona either stayed in with her or else invited her out with her friends. Some weeks later, after a late evening in the library, Shona had gone for a drink with a class-mate. When she returned to her room later that night she found that her room-mate had cut her arms again. The sight of her room-mate's blood-streaked arms had filled her with a mixture of emotions including rage, helplessness, guilt and pity and, unable to contain her feelings any longer, she had burst into tears. The following day, Shona told her tutor that she could no longer cope with her room-mate and wanted him to support her request for a change of accommodation. In this case, the communication, possibly unconscious, underlying her room-mate's cutting was, 'if you leave me alone, I will cut my arms'; and it was this demand, with its accompanying threat, that eventually became intolerable to Shona.

As with students who are considered to be suicidal or at risk of psychological breakdown, the question arises as to what might constitute a reasonable response in the face of such destructive behaviour. Unlike students who are intent on suicide or breakdown, however, the risk of serious immediate injury through self-harming behaviours is usually much less. There is, therefore, more space for thinking about the reasons underlying the student's behaviour – on the counsellor's part at least – and a more measured response may be possible. What is obviously missing for the student who *acts* self-destructively under the sway of intense emotional conflict is the capacity to contain and think about their feelings. As already stated, deeper levels of psychological disturbance are characterised by a failure in symbolism and a regression to primitive modes of emotional expression. Under these circumstances, the primary aim of the counsellor, therefore, is the promotion of thinking as opposed to acting and this has implications for the involvement of other agencies such as psychiatric services. One of the difficulties for counsellors and others in dealing with students who self-harm is that their behaviour, designed to relieve their own anxiety, often arouses a great deal of anxiety in other people associated with them. As a result, there may be additional pressure upon the counsellor from family and friends to take some action to stop the student's self-harming behaviour. In this way, the climate surrounding the student can rapidly become one that favours action and is hostile to thinking, making the task of understanding what is driving the student's self-harming behaviour even more difficult. This is not to say that no action should be taken, indeed psychiatric assessment with the provision of appropriate treatment can sometimes be a most helpful way forward, rather it is to emphasise the need for *thoughtful action*. In many instances, self-harming behaviour that is not too extreme is a temporary, if desperate, measure. If it can be adequately contained within the counselling process, with or without the support of other agencies, and its defensive purpose in the student's psychological armoury explored, *whether or not* its meaning is fully apprehended, there is a good likelihood of its passing in favour of a more benign symptom. Where precipitate action interferes with the opportunity for thinking, and therefore development, self-harming behaviours may become more entrenched and intractable.

The university setting

When a student develops a serious mental illness or attempts suicide at university, especially if this happens in the period before important examinations, questions inevitably arise as to whether too much pressure was put upon the student academically, whether adequate pastoral support was available, whether tutors were sufficiently alert to the student's well-being, and so on. There is a sense of failure on the part of the university and a feeling of having let the student down; and it is right and proper that the university should reflect upon, and learn from, these sad experiences. Less obvious, however, are the many ways in which universities do in fact successfully support and foster the development of individuals who are not yet emotionally prepared to face the world without the familiar structures of home, family and school and who might otherwise break down or collapse under the ordinary demands of adult life. Karen, described at the beginning of this chapter, is an example of just such an individual and her story illustrates the invaluable contribution that universities can make towards the development of a young person whose psychological problems are particularly severe. In Karen's case, she was encouraged to develop a relationship with her department, focused largely, though not exclusively, on one or two key members, which contained several essential features. In the first place, her department had confidence in her academic abilities; secondly, they were willing to be flexible in their response to unpredictable changes in her emotional state; thirdly, and as an important balance in their accommodation of her, they were robust in their demands of her as a student; fourthly, they directed her to the university counselling service and, with her agreement, established contact with her counsellor; and fifthly, they ensured that, within reason, there would always be a member of the department, whom she could contact. It will be obvious that the conditions set up by Karen's department, in conjunction with the counselling service, approximated to that of a supportive family and this was, essentially, what Karen needed in order to be able to continue her development. Although her relationships with both her department and her counsellor were put under enormous strain by her and, at times, it seemed as though they might not withstand her assaults on them, nor weather her neglect of them, they were maintained and provided her with the structure she needed in order to continue with her development. As she approached her final year, it became clear that she had begun to internalise an experience of having her feelings contained by this quasi-family. This was manifest in a notable decrease in her suspiciousness of those trying to help her as she became more able to use their advice and support. Further evidence of her internalisation of a containing relationship which would help her to deal more effectively with her feelings was to be found towards the end of the year in her successful management of her intense feelings of anxiety prior to her final examinations. While it would not be true to say that her experience as a student at university had 'cured' Karen of her psychological illness, it would be fair to say that she had made significant gains in her emotional development that might not have otherwise been possible. After leaving university she was able to live independently, requiring only outpatient psychiatric support, an outcome that had seemed impossible when she began at university.

The primary aim of universities is not, of course, therapeutic, their purpose lies elsewhere, in the fields of research and education. However, the atmosphere of the university is one which encourages thinking and the cultivation of understanding and, as such, it is conducive to psychological growth and development. For some students, such as Karen, whose previous life experiences have failed to equip them adequately for adulthood, university may provide a second chance to develop some of the tools they will need later in life.

Further reading

Anderson, R. and Dartington, A. (eds) (1998) *Facing It Out: Clinical Perspectives on Adolescent Disturbance*, London: Duckworth.

Laufer, M. (ed.) (1995) *The Suicidal Adolescent*, London: Karnac Books.

Laufer, M. and Laufer, E. (1984) *Adolescence and Developmental Breakdown*, New Haven: Yale University Press.

8

THE UNIVERSITY CONTEXT

An eminent psychoanalyst wrote about her treatment of an adolescent girl whose highly disturbing behaviour had suggested a possible diagnosis of schizophrenia. The girl was seen five times a week for about two years and improved considerably. A year or so later, at a chance meeting, the girl told her analyst, 'I feel I have paid a heavy price for my treatment. Not with money, but I am always with older people nowadays. I assume I have matured during my treatment somehow – but like a plant that might grow too quickly in a hot-house.' Her analyst agreed with her and wrote, 'I consider that her analysis may have led to a foreclosure of adolescence resulting in pseudo-adaptation to adulthood.'

M. Tonnesmann, 1980

My purpose in quoting the above is *not* to decry the value or importance of intensive psychotherapeutic or psychoanalytic treatment for young people. For a small, but significant, number of adolescents such treatment is entirely appropriate and may be necessary in order for them to continue their emotional development with any measure of success. In such cases, development of mature independence without help is not an option and the possibility of a second chance to achieve independence from within a therapeutic 'dependent' relationship is essential; sadly, it is rarely available. Rather, my point is to emphasise that the force that drives the process of adolescence forward is the young person's struggle for independence from his parents and away from his infantile dependence upon them; therapy, especially if it is intensive or prolonged, implies a continuing dependence and, as such, runs counter to the forward developmental flow of adolescence. It could be argued, therefore, that the counsellor's primary aim with students, the majority of whom are in the latter stages of adolescence, should be to encourage and support them in their strivings towards independence rather than to foster their regressive tendencies towards infantile dependence upon the counsellor. Of course, as already stated, there are students whose capacity for relationships has been so severely damaged or restricted that the establishment of a therapeutic relationship in which they can become dependent is a significant achievement; as well as an essential prerequisite to their subsequent emotional development. To return to the quotation above, however, the point was not that the girl did not require help, she certainly did, rather it was to question the appropriateness of the help she received at that time in her life, *bearing in mind that she was an adolescent*. Might a different kind of approach have enabled her to have reached adult-hood at a lesser cost?

For the counsellor who is confronted with a student who is both disturbed and disturbing in his behaviour, there is often pressure from others affected by the student – teaching staff, family, and others – to act in order to defuse the situation. Gathering the student and all his messy adolescent strivings up into the relative containment of an ongoing therapy may well reduce the level of anxiety in himself and in those around him. However, it may also deprive him of the necessary tension to push on and work through the adolescent conflicts exhibited in his difficult behaviour and towards adulthood. Obviously, in the context of the university, there is a balance to be struck between what the student might need to express to advance his emotional development and that which the institution can tolerate. Universities are not, after all, hospitals or even treatment centres; though some therapeutic activity may go on in a university, they are institutions for the advancement of education. It is reasonable, therefore, for universi-ties to demand a certain minimum level of academic function from students and to require that students who are unable to meet these minimal requirements leave. Within this context, the aim of most counselling in universities is to enable and support students, in the broadest sense, in the pursuance of these requirements while they are at university. In some circumstances, this may include helping them to leave or, perhaps, to defer their studies for some time. Thus, among several factors delimiting the acceptability of a student's behaviour, their capacity to carry on with their studies is paramount.

In this chapter we will be looking at the nature of the counselling work that is done in universities and how the parameters of the institution influence this.

Counselling within universities

Most university counselling departments offer a variety of services which may include brief or short-term counselling; longer-term counselling or psychotherapy; group counselling or psychotherapy; and psychiatric assessment. Some also provide groups with a specific and limited focus, for example, study skills, relaxation skills and so on. The factors which influence and determine the nature of services provided are diverse and, for the sake of discussion, can be roughly divided into two interactive sets, those which emanate from the needs of the students and those which are driven by the parameters of the university. Sometimes these come into conflict. For instance, a number of universities require that foreign language students spend a year abroad, studying or working, in order to improve their language skills. This requirement may preclude the possibility of, or may even interrupt, ongoing counselling or therapy for some students for whom it might be considered advisable.

The needs of the student; short-term counselling

The major part of this book has been concerned with the emotional needs of the student at university with particular reference to the demands of late adolescence. Throughout, the primacy of the struggle towards independence and the evolution of a personal sense of identity have been emphasised and, earlier in this chapter, the potential foreclosure of this process by the introduction of intensive therapy was touched upon. With these themes in mind, it was further suggested that the 'ideal' intervention with the majority of students might be one that supported and fostered the ongoing process of adolescence with dependence on the counsellor kept to a necessary minimum. However, before exploring further how this might be provided, there is another factor to consider, namely the importance of responding swiftly to requests for help from students.

Most students seek counselling when a crisis point is reached, that is, when they cannot find a way of moving forward on their own and they recognise that they are in need of help. In these circumstances, a fast response to their needs is important and, if timely, a brief period of counselling is often sufficient to get them back 'on track'. If they have to wait too long for help, perhaps because there is a lengthy waiting list, they may give up and withdraw, taking with them an experience of their efforts to obtain help having been frustrated. Of course, no counselling service can expect to provide instant access. However, tolerance levels among adolescents are much lower than among adults and this has to be borne in mind in the design and provision of counselling services for students. Counselling that is accessible when the student wants and needs it is much more likely to be effective than that which comes available weeks later, not least because of the more ready access to feelings which have not yet been obscured by a host of defences. In determining what constitutes a reasonable response time, the structure of the university's academic year as well as the timing of the student's request for help have both to be taken into account. For example, a student who was studying away from home at a university that had a conventional three term structure went to his counselling service for help in the penultimate week of his second term. He intended returning to his family home at the end of the term and had become extremely anxious about the exams he had to sit on his return four weeks later. In this case, the student was going home in less than two weeks. An appointment was therefore needed within that time, preferably with sufficient leeway for a follow-up appointment if necessary. This type of scenario, where a student comes for help at the last minute before exams, is a familiar one to counsellors and reflects the intensely ambivalent attitude of many students to their need for help; asking for help may be felt as tantamount to personal failure. (In coming forward for help close to the end of the second term, when most counselling services are hard pressed to meet the demands upon them, a student may be enacting any number of unconscious dynamics including an inability to think beyond his own needs. The inability, or refusal, to think about the needs of others, their total self-preoccupation, is characteristic of adolescents and contributes to much of the conflict between parents and adolescent children and is repeated in the sorts of logistical problems described above.) Recognising the urgency with which many students present themselves as well as the importance of meeting this need, the majority of university counselling services do in fact offer a rapid response whereby a student will be seen for an initial appointment within a week or two. Further appointments will depend on the structure of the counselling service and on the type of counselling offered.

Returning to the issue of what type of counselling might be best suited to the needs of the majority of students who seek counselling, it is generally accepted that brief, or short-term, counselling is the most appropriate form of intervention. As to how many sessions constitute 'brief' or 'short-term' counselling, this is locally determined by individual counselling services and usually describes an intervention of between one and ten sessions. Several factors suggest that short-term counselling of this duration is appropriate for most students. For instance, annual reports from many counselling services record that the average number of sessions *attended* by individual students is invariably four or five, irrespective of the number offered. Also, the proposal of a brief time-limited period of counselling is less likely to stimulate anxieties about becoming dependent on a counsellor; by the same token, the student's potential tendencies in the direction of increased dependence are discouraged.

'Short-term counselling' is a general term which describes a number of different activities that are more or less therapeutic in aim. They can be loosely grouped into four overlapping categories: clarification; catharsis; assessment, the outcome of which may be a recommendation for short-term psychodynamic counselling, referral for longer-term psychotherapy or, in some cases, referral for psychiatric assessment; and short-term psychodynamic counselling. While the following examples have been chosen to highlight these different aspects of short-term counselling, it is important to keep in mind that all four activities usually play some part in each short-term counselling intervention. The first example illustrates how a brief series of counselling sessions, in this case one session, was helpful in clarifying a particular problem.

Chris began his first counselling session with the words, 'I'm not quite sure where to start.' He went on to describe in detail a heated row with his girlfriend during the previous week and how it had continued to play on his mind, making it impossible for him to concentrate on his work. He interspersed his account of their row with questions as to what the counsellor thought his girlfriend had meant by certain statements she had made. The counsellor eventually observed that he might find this out himself by speaking to his girlfriend. Chris replied that he could not speak to his girlfriend since it was she who had started the row and that it was therefore up to her to make the first contact; he added that she might think him weak otherwise. Picking up Chris' anxiety, the counsellor commented that he seemed very worried about losing face with his girlfriend. Chris responded to this reflection of his feelings by confiding that this was his first 'proper' relationship and that he was afraid of making a mess of things and that his friends had said that he should wait for his girlfriend to ring him. The counsellor now suggested that perhaps Chris was more concerned about his friends' opinion than that of his girlfriend. Chris thought that maybe he had been more worried about what his friends would think. Then he asked the counsellor if he thought that he should ring his girlfriend. The counsellor recalled Chris' earlier concern about 'making a mess of things' and suggested that perhaps Chris was afraid of deciding for himself, in case things turned out badly. In response, Chris began to put forward reasons why he should ring his girlfriend.

In this example, we can see how gradual clarification of Chris' feelings, in the context of the problem he brings, enables him to shift from 'not [being] quite sure where to start' to a position where he can begin to think about how to resolve his current problem. In this case, no attempt was made to explore the deeper dynamics underlying Chris' anxieties, rather the focus of the counselling was on helping Chris clarify his present problem.

Catharsis refers to the process by which relief is obtained through being able to ventilate one's feelings (and is particularly encouraged in, for example, the funeral rituals of some cultures). It does not aim to investigate unconscious dynamics and the emphasis is on emotional relief in the here-and-now and a restoration of equilibrium. There is no working through of internal issues and, consequently, no change at a psychic level; thus, the individual is no better prepared to deal with these same feelings when assailed by them again in the future. While catharsis is, therefore, of limited therapeutic value it can sometimes provide a temporary period of respite. In the following example, we can see how the opportunity to express her feelings to a counsellor helped one student to manage powerful feelings of homesickness in the context of a disappointing initial experience of life away from home.

Jasmin had been 'sent' to see a counsellor by her tutor to whom she had confided her intense feelings of homesickness. She had been considering transferring to a university in her home town in order that she could return to live with her parents. Paradoxically, Jasmin's choice of university had been informed by her wish to leave home and she had been eagerly looking forward to the experience of living with other young people in a big city. She had grown up in a small country town and although she had a happy home life she had felt the need to stretch her wings and she had come to university in a spirit of confidence and expectation. Unfortunately, a number of problems had beset her on her arrival at university. First, her halls of residence were still undergoing redecoration and, along with the other students in her halls, she had been temporarily housed in rather unpleasant bed and breakfast accommodation for her first three weeks. Secondly, she found living in a big city overwhelming and a very different experience from her previous brief visits to the city. Thirdly, she missed her friends from home badly and, partly because of her accommodation problems, had not managed to make friends with other students yet. Finally, her course was a lot more difficult than she had imagined it would be and she was beginning to feel that she would not be able to keep up.

In her first counselling session she cried as all her frustrations and disappointments spilled out and she seemed, at times, inconsolable and as if the only solution was for her to go home. She had spoken to her parents who were sympathetic but had encouraged her to stay until half-term, another two weeks hence. She had reluctantly agreed and although she was sure that she would want to return home at half-term she agreed to a further two counselling sessions. At her next counselling session, her mood was perceptibly lighter and though she was adamant about leaving university the following week, she talked with animation about a party she had been to with some new friends from her corridor in her halls of residence. She was also planning an evening out to a nightclub with them at the weekend. She was still finding her course work difficult but had discovered that others in her class were struggling too and that had reassured her somewhat. She cried when she talked about missing her family and friends at home but was much less tearful than during the previous session. As in the previous session, her counsellor acknowledged how difficult she was finding everything and how much she was missing all the support she had at home. Jasmin came to her next and 'last' session in a cheerful mood having had a lively weekend. She was still looking forward to going home for half-term but now she intended coming back afterwards. She was again tearful when she spoke about her family and friends at home and wondered if she would ever get over missing them so much. At the end of the session she asked her counsellor if she could come back for another session after the half-term break. At this next session Jasmin reported a very enjoyable half-term catching up with her friends and seeing her family. She had had mixed feelings about coming back to university but had been looking forward to seeing her new friends again and, on the whole, was pleased to be back. As the session came to a close Jasmin asked her counsellor if she needed to come back. Her counsellor suggested that they might meet again in a fortnight and that she could get in touch again beforehand if she needed to. A couple of days before this meeting, Jasmin cancelled her appointment. She left a message thanking her counsellor for his help and saying that she felt fine now and hoped that it would be all right for her to see him again in the future if she felt that she needed to.

In this example, Jasmin was seen for four sessions altogether. Over that period she used her counselling sessions to express her feelings of anger, frustration, helplessness and so forth and this relief enabled her to remain at university. The difficulties she experienced with her accommodation certainly exacerbated her problems, however, it seemed likely that she would have struggled with acute homesickness nevertheless. Her counsellor was aware of her strong desire for independence and his interventions were directed towards supporting this. He did not, therefore, encourage her to continue with counselling when it seemed that she might manage on her own and actively 'weaned' her off with his suggestion of a two week break between sessions.

Assessment constitutes the third arm of short-term counselling and forms part of every short-term counselling intervention. It may be a more or less intensive process, depending on the nature and severity of the problem that is presented and also on what further counselling or therapy is under consideration. In the two examples described above, the counsellor's assessment of each student and his or her situation, was relatively superficial. Chris and Jasmin both presented well-defined problems that they wished immediate help with and neither conveyed a sense of wanting to examine their problems in more depth. In the next example, the counsellor's assessment leads to a very different outcome.

A counsellor was initially struck by the vehemence of a student's complaints about his friends. Upon hearing the student's story about how badly he had been treated by his friends, his counsellor considered that the student's complaints about his friends did, at face value, appear to be justified and that the behaviour of his friends had been extremely unreasonable given the circumstances described by the student. However, when the counsellor tried to understand more about the situation by deepening his discussion with the student, the student became hostile and accused the counsellor of doubting him. This enabled the counsellor to reach the hypothesis that the student's complaints were more likely indicative of paranoid thinking on the student's part than that his friends were engaged conspiratorially against him; he also thought that the student would be unlikely to concur with this view. The student was strongly disinclined to thinking more openly about his feelings, rather he wanted the counsellor to endorse his thinking and to agree completely with him that his friends were malevolently disposed towards him. Far from being helpful, another point of view was experienced by this student as a threat to his psychological integrity and, therefore, to be resisted at all costs.

Where there is such a discrepancy in perception between student and counsellor, as in this case, the likelihood of finding a common focus for counselling is limited. The counsellor's assessment, therefore, was that short-term exploratory counselling would not be advisable for this student and that a psychiatric referral might be one possible option, although it seemed unlikely that the student would be willing to consider this.

In Chapter 7 where we explored the areas of psychosis, suicide and self-harm, the importance of assessing potential levels of risk and further therapeutic needs was self-evident. Where there is no such immediate risk, assessment is still necessary in order to determine the most appropriate intervention and, in some cases, may be the main focus of the counselling intervention. The following two examples illustrate this different emphasis. The first concerns a student who began to suffer from panic attacks while at university and who was able to make effective use of short-term psychodynamic counselling, the fourth type of short-term counselling, while the second deals with a student with a long-standing eating disorder who clearly required longer term therapy. In both cases, issues beyond the student's presenting problem were taken up by the counsellor in order that he could make an assessment of the *internal dynamics* underlying the explicit problem. Of course, the student's ability to make use of a particular type of therapy, as well as his interest in pursuing it, were also important considerations in the assessment.

Will had been experiencing panic attacks for about a month before he saw a counsellor. He did not know why they had started or what precipitated each attack and he had grown afraid that they might not stop. Normally a confident young man, he had been badly shaken by these inexplicable bouts of anxiety. His account of his first attack, which occurred while he was watching TV during a weekend visit home, was apparently unremarkable and shed no light on the source of his intense anxiety. The circumstances of his subsequent panic attacks were equally unilluminating. His description of the discussion within his family about his panic attacks suggested that his family was concerned and supportive. He was now in his second year at university and though not entirely up to date with his course work, he was reasonably satisfied with his progress. As with the other areas of his life, his social life seemed relatively unproblematic. After Will had repeated his description of the circumstances of his first panic attack, the counsellor asked if anything else had occurred at home during that weekend. He replied that he couldn't recall anything special about that weekend but that the previous Saturday, Honey, the family dog, had been involved in a nasty car accident and he and his father had taken Honey to the vet to have her foot amputated; his mother had been too upset to go with them. He added that Honey had made a good recovery and was now getting used to going about on three legs. It emerged that Honey had been given to Will on his thirteenth birthday and had been 'his' dog until he came to university; also, that he was very fond of Honey. The counsellor was consequently struck by Will's apparent equanimity at the time of Honey's terrible injury and also that this event came to the fore when Will was asked about his first panic attack. He asked him if he thought that Honey's accident might have anything to do with his panic attacks. Will replied, 'Do you think it might?'

In this case, the counsellor wondered if Honey's accident might have stirred up repressed thoughts and feelings associated with the event and that Will's panic attacks might be symptomatic of his fear of these becoming conscious. There were no other obvious current areas of conflict. In addition, Will did not discount the possibility of a link between his panic attacks and Honey's accident, and he expressed interest in understanding the origins of his panic attacks. These were among the factors that contributed to the counsellor's assessment that Will might benefit from short-term psychodynamic counselling focused on exploring the unconscious feelings associated with Honey's accident.

Incidentally, one of the problems that may occur in short-term counselling of this type is that of excessive idealisation of the counsellor. There are many potential reasons for this phenomenon which commonly represents a defence against strong unconscious negative feelings. While idealisation is a typical feature of the transference relationship in longer-term counselling and therapy, there is limited scope in short-term work for understanding and resolving it. It is therefore preferable in brief counselling to discourage potential idealisation, for instance, by the counsellor explaining how he came to arrive at a particular observation or interpretation. This has the dual benefit of demystifying the counselling process as well as modelling a different way of thinking for the student.

The next example describes an assessment in which the counsellor considered that the severity of the problems presented by the

student, and the student's ability to make use of psychological interpretation, together indicated that longer term psychotherapy might
be of most help to this student.

A first year biology student, Sonia, had been struggling with an
eating disorder for several years before coming to university. In her
first meeting, she talked at length about her brother whom she
portrayed as overly dependent upon their mother. Her brother had
sufered from a series of minor health problems as a child and, as a
result, had often missed school. Unlike his sister, he showed scant
interest in his school work and eventually left with poor A-level
grades. He was now unemployed and living at home with their
mother who complained incessantly to Sonia about his failure to get
a job. Sonia's frustration with her mother, whom she felt did little to
discourage her brother's passivity and dependence upon her, was
barely disguised. As if to emphasise the contrast between herself
and her brother, Sonia added that her mother often remarked on
how Sonia had never given her any trouble and that she had always
been 'a perfect child'. Sonia was offered five sessions which she
gratefully accepted. Over the course of the first three sessions she
appeared to gain a great deal of understanding and she was eager
and willing to face up to a lot of difficult and potentially painful
things about herself. She herself felt she was learning a lot about
herself and she considered that a very good start; after all, as she
told her counsellor, she didn't expect miracles. Sonia's re-enactment
in her relationship with the counsellor of the dynamics between
herself and her mother, in which any signs of open conflict were
glaringly absent, was plain to see. Just as she had been the perfect,
uncomplaining child, now she was the perfect, undemanding
patient. However, in the penultimate session there was a change in
her mood. She expressed a pessimism about relationships ever lasting and confided her belief that she would end up with a series of
broken relationships. She thought she would never be able to find
someone who would be able to give her what she wanted. In
response to this her counsellor raised the issue of the impending
ending of their sessions. Sonia replied that she had felt 'a little bit
angry' but realised that, 'oh well ... nothing ever lasts'.
Acknowledging her disappointment, her counsellor indicated that
she thought that longer term therapy would be helpful for her and
offered to help her find a suitable therapist. When Sonia returned for
her final session she was able to tell her counsellor that she had felt
angry and upset when she had left the previous session. She had felt
it was unfair that things didn't last and had felt like bingeing.

However, on this occasion she had been able to resist the temptation to binge. Sonia's not bingeing was eventually understood in terms of her having been able to experience her anger and disappointment and bring it back to her counsellor, rather than express it via bingeing.

In this example, the counsellor was aware from the outset that Sonia's eating disorder was longstanding and that she would need longer term help. Assessment of the nature of Sonia's problems and, crucially, her readiness for longer term therapy were, consequently, to the fore in the counsellor's mind. The counsellor therefore took note of, but did not delve deeply into, the major problematic emotional areas in Sonia's world including jealousy of her brother, feelings about her father who was significant by his total absence from her story, ambivalent feelings towards her mother, and so on. However the counsellor did take up directly Sonia's feelings about the end of her counselling sessions and being passed on, in a way that was both therapeutically helpful and useful for the assessment. The counsellor's interpretation of Sonia's pessimism about relationships as a defence against her angry feelings towards the counsellor, helped Sonia to feel understood and to think about these feelings; at the same time, the counsellor was able to assess Sonia's capacity to make use of this form of help. Sonia's ability to hold on to and talk about her feelings, as opposed to bingeing, at her next session suggested that she might benefit significantly from longer term psychodynamic therapy.

Aside from short-term or brief counselling, the other mainstay of student counselling is group counselling or group therapy. A proper account of group therapy and its application in student counselling is beyond the scope of this book and only a few brief remarks will be included here. Interested readers will find references for further reading in this area at the end of this chapter. As with individual counselling or therapy, group therapy may also be short term but is more commonly of a longer duration, lasting between six months and a year. While group therapy can be extremely effective for some students, it is not appropriate for everyone and a careful assessment of suitability is necessary before an individual is recommended for a group. Also, it is generally considered important that individual group members should confine *all* their communications with one another to their group sessions; as a result, a group is unlikely to admit a new member who knows existing members of that group. The need to maintain this level of anonymity between members outside of the group is obviously more difficult to achieve in a relatively closed community such as a university where individuals live and work closely together.

Institutional parameters

The nature of counselling within universities is heavily influenced by the parameters of the institution, the most obvious of which are temporal. In recent years some universities have shifted away from the traditional structure of the academic year, comprising of three terms of varying lengths amounting to around thirty weeks in all. However, most have retained this basic format and our discussion will reflect this. Other institutional factors that we will consider include *placements*, that is, where students are required, as part of their course, to spend a certain amount of time away from the university, for example, a year abroad developing their language skills, or to engage in a practical application such as an archaeological dig. We will also look at how examinations affect counselling provision and, finally, the implications for counselling of the institution as a 'closed environment'.

Temporal factors

For the majority of students, the academic year begins in the autumn and is divided into three terms. Each term has its own character, determined by factors both within and without the university, which is discernible in the different types of problems that students present during the three terms. Not surprisingly, a greater number of students come for counselling during the first term with problems such as homesickness and depression, especially students in their first year. Another problem, sometimes related to that of homesickness, that is more common in the first term arises when a student is unhappy or disappointed with their choice of course or university but has little idea about what alternative they might prefer. Problems of loneliness and difficulties in making new friends are also frequent during the first term. Difficulties in keeping up with course work and anxieties about falling behind are also typical of the first term and often reflect the very different nature of university and school teaching; the relative lack of structure and need for self-motivation require an adjustment that a number of students find hard to make. For many of these students, a brief series of counselling sessions, with an emphasis on supporting them while they find their feet, is often sufficient; group counselling or therapy can be particularly effective for some of these students in that it provides a degree of peer support and affirmation. As evident in the case of Jasmin, described above, a fast response is of paramount importance for students who are on the verge of giving up. Towards the end of the first term many of these problems of settling in are beginning to be resolved and a different set of problems arises. As Christmas approaches, 'party season' begins and problems associated with relationships, both with family and friends, become more prominent. Students in the latter years of their course may be torn between spending Christmas and New Year with their family and with their friends. Parents often expect their children to return home for Christmas and can feel very hurt when they choose to go elsewhere, particularly if they spend Christmas with a friend's family. Many students' parents have separated or divorced by the time they come to university and the student may be faced with a painful dilemma about where to spend Christmas. Some students are unable to visit their families for practical reasons such as geographical distance, while for others the distance is an emotional one. For a significant number of students, the emphasis on Christmas as a family occasion can be an especially painful and depressing reminder of their own family problems. In a similar vein, students who are already on the fringe socially can feel even more left out and isolated from the hectic socialising that goes on in the weeks before Christmas. Most university counselling services remain open for some time between the first and second terms and the continuation of their counselling during this period can be of enormous help to students who would otherwise find themselves without support.

The character of the second term, especially the latter part, is largely determined by the imminence of exams in the third term. Pressures of work are also behind the anxieties of students who neglected or fell behind with their academic work in the first term and who are now struggling to catch up. Symptoms associated with high levels of anxiety such as panic attacks are more common as deadlines for essays and projects approach. Students who, despite being well ahead with their work, desperately want to excel in the next term's exams may feel unable to contain their anxiety and come for help. For example, women with eating disorders, who have been trying to maintain control over their emotional world by controlling their food, may find that they are no longer able to control their anxiety in this way. Students who come for counselling in a state of panic are often not in an appropriate frame of mind to think about their problems in a reflective way. Heightened states of anxiety can be accompanied by very distressing and frightening physical symptoms and leave little room for any thought other than a wish for an immediate release from their symptoms. Confronted with a panic-stricken student, the counsellor may feel under pressure to act, to do something immediate to relieve the student's anxiety, for example, by referring the student to a doctor for medication to reduce their anxiety. (While psychotropic medication can be helpful under certain circumstances and after careful assessment, it is rarely helpful as an immediate response to anxiety when it is more likely to confirm the individual's fear that his anxiety is not bearable.) Under such conditions, it is important for the counsellor to maintain his ability to think and to desist from acting, at least until he has been able to reach some understanding of the student's anxiety. Often the counsellor's capacity to contain the anxiety aroused in him by the student, and to continue to think with him about what is going on, is experienced by the student as containing, resulting in a diminution in his level of anxiety and, hopefully, a commensurate increase in his ability to think.

The problems that students bring during the third term are not uncommonly concerned with issues about endings. The long summer break entails the dissolution of student households and friendships which may or may not survive over the summer vacation and this casts a depressive air over the final term, especially after the emotional intensity surrounding the exam period has passed. Anxieties about the future beyond university are also to the fore. For students in their final year, disappointment about their degree class along with regrets for not having worked harder are not unusual. And for those who are leaving university, the excitement of entering the adult world of work and independence may be tempered with sadness about leaving the last vestiges of adolescence behind. Of course, some students who are not yet ready for the responsibilities of adulthood stall and enrol as postgraduates!

As discussed above, much of the work done in student counselling is short term and is, preferably, encompassed within one term. The long breaks between terms, along with half-term breaks in some universities, make ongoing weekly counselling a difficult process to sustain out of term time, especially with students living away from home. The long summer break is particularly inimical to continuing counselling from one academic year to the next and is more often feasible with postgraduate students who have much shorter holidays. These temporal restrictions, together with the emphasis on promoting independence in students who are occupied with the developmental issues of late adolescence, give student counselling a more direct focus than would be the case in general adult counselling and inform the style of counselling accordingly.

Placements

Many language courses require their students to spend a year abroad, either enrolled as a student in a university or else engaged in some suitable employment, for example, as an assistant teacher in a school, the general aim being to improve and develop their language skills. While, at its best, this can be an enriching and enjoyable experience some students experience difficulties and are unable to fulfil their course requirements. In some cases inadequate forward planning of the placement is clearly a major factor in the failure of the placement, in others the problems appear to be more a consequence of the student's emotional unreadiness for such an experience. Many students who return prematurely from their year abroad cite loneliness and homesickness as their main reasons for coming home early. Often the placement fails because of a combination of these two factors as in the following example.

Maria returned home from her year abroad in Spain after only three weeks because of extreme homesickness. She and a friend from her course had chosen the option of studying together in a small college in the north of Spain. Unfortunately, her friend had developed glandular fever a fortnight before they were due to leave and had been unable to go. After she had come back, Maria became depressed and her tutor suggested that she attend the counselling service. In the course of her counselling it emerged that, when they had learned that her friend would not be going to Spain, Maria's family had tried to dissuade her from going. However, Maria had been determined to go, even on her own. The youngest of three children, she described herself disparagingly as 'the baby of the family' and, when her family had urged her not to go to Spain alone, she had experienced their concern as evidence of the family's view of her as incapable of looking after herself. For Maria, going to Spain had become a concrete expression of her struggle for independence in which her difficulties with separation were denied; thus, her fear of being faced with her need for others made her unable to consider her family's concerns. Her failure to manage the separation confirmed that, *at an internal level*, she had not yet managed to establish an independent self, and this had been a major factor in her subsequent depression.

A forthcoming placement may lead to the premature closure of an ongoing period of counselling or therapy. While this is unfortunate, if issues related to the ending can be faced and worked through, then this experience can help to prepare the student for the separation (from family, friends, university and so forth) that his placement will entail. If, on the other hand, the individual is not yet ready to deal with these issues, then there may be an increase in defences which may include denial of painful feelings and/or an intensification of excited feelings about the imminent placement. Such difficulties in acknowledging feelings associated with separation can undermine the student's subsequent adaptation in his placement.

Placements of different kinds are required by various university courses. As mentioned above, some archaeology courses require their students to gain experience on archaeological sites abroad as well as at home and although this is generally for a much shorter length of time, some students nevertheless encounter difficulties in meeting the requirements. One young man who suffered from extreme social anxiety was terrified at the prospect of having to share dormitory accommodation on one such trip. Many of the problems associated with placements are related to difficulties in managing separations. Where these are not severe, support and encouragement may be sufficient. However, where problems are more extensive, as in Maria's case, a period of therapy may be needed.

Examinations

Although some university departments have moved over wholly or in part to a continuous assessment system of evaluation, exams still occupy a significant part of the academic year in most universities. The majority of examinations take place during the final summer term and much of the work of student counselling during this time is coloured by this fact even when anxiety about exams is not the primary focus. Minds become crammed with revision and there is little spare room for reflection about other issues, however important. Some students use counselling during this time as a repository for anxieties about other aspects of their lives that they cannot manage while working for exams, as if depositing them with the counsellor will free their mind to concentrate on their work. For others the counsellor is cast in a more overtly parental role and the student may move into a more dependent position, asking for advice on revision strategies, the benefits or otherwise of certain exam techniques and so on. The wish to be looked after while they take their exams is plainly evident in the large numbers of students who return to live in their parental homes prior to examinations. Some openly admit to wanting to be looked after – their meals cooked, their clothes washed, and so on – while others feel more able to concentrate at home away from the potential distraction of their friends. Other more anxious students find the generally heightened atmosphere of anxiety around the period of exams debilitating while others cannot bear the competitiveness that pervades this time. One student, in her final year, could not enter the university libraries around exam time because she would see the same people still there in the evening that she had seen in the morning and she was sure that they must be doing so much more work than she was. She would weep copiously during her counselling sessions about how other people were doing much more work than she was despite the fact that she had a draconian revision timetable that began at 8 a.m. and continued until 10 p.m. with only four half-hour breaks. She was insistent that she only wanted to pass and it was only after she had her results and was sure that she had obtained a first class degree that she was able to admit to how much she had wanted to beat everyone else. As with many other students, it was impossible for this student to think about anything beyond her next exam during this period. This preoccupation is not uncommon and most students' minds are filled with the exams they have to sit and this has to be taken into account in their counselling. Indeed, a student who displays no anxiety about forthcoming exams is more likely to give cause for concern. A certain amount of anxiety is generally helpful in focusing the student on his work and a student who does not express any anxiety about imminent exams may be out of touch with his feelings. For example, a geography student came for counselling a fortnight before his second year exams. He had consulted his doctor because of severe headaches in the previous two weeks. His doctor had diagnosed tension headaches and advised him to see a counsellor. He could think of no reason for his headaches and though he had done very little work for his forthcoming exams he appeared unconcerned about failing them. Under the circumstances it seemed not unlikely that his headaches were the physical manifestation of dissociated anxieties about his exams.

In the period after the examinations and while results are coming through, there is a good deal of variation in the mood of the students who come to counselling sessions. There is apprehension among those awaiting results, relief for those who have got the results they needed, joy for those who have exceeded their own expectations and disappointment for others who have not reached their targets. Many, however, share a sense of emptiness that fills the space previously occupied by the manic activity of the preceding weeks of revision and examinations. Along with the sadness that inevitably accompanies the end of the year, this can precipitate feelings of deep depression in some students. For the majority, however, this is a temporary phase and freedom from academic work and the summer ahead are generally sufficient to lift their mood.

The 'closed' environment and confidentiality

Universities are, in an important sense with respect to the counselling that they provide, a relatively 'closed' environment and this is especially so of campus universities where students live and work in close physical proximity to one another. The main implication of this for counselling is that protection of confidentiality is a more complex issue than might be the case for counselling in a more general setting. Most student counselling services operate a policy of confidentiality within their services which means that a student's contact with the service is confidential to the service unless the student gives his permission otherwise. The importance of maintaining this level of confidentiality can be very difficult for other staff in the university to grasp and this applies particularly to teaching staff who may be worried about a student whom they have referred to the counselling service. Parents also often find it hard to understand why they cannot be kept informed about their children, especially when they have particular reason for concern. Both parents and staff alike may not see why basic information such as whether or not their child or student has attended the counselling service cannot be divulged. While their frustration and anger is certainly understandable, the capacity to maintain confidentiality remains at the heart of a viable counselling service and many students, arguably those most in need of help, would not come forward for help if the service was not strictly confidential. Most counsellors would encourage students who are in serious difficulties to speak to their family and to their tutors, but their primary responsibility is to the student and they would not make counselling contingent upon this. There are, of course, exceptional circumstances when a counsellor might breach confidentiality, for instance if the life of the student or others was seriously in danger, but this is a rare occurrence and in most instances the permission of the student would be sought. Part of the difficulty for parents and for staff, who are in a quasi-parental position in relation to students, is that students, albeit legally adults in most cases, occupy a position that is still emotionally between that of child and adult. When a student is experiencing problems both parents and staff become anxious and understandably want to act, to do something, to protect their child, as the student is now seen, as well as to relieve their own anxiety. When the student resists their involvement and their efforts to help they may become frustrated and angry and this is often redirected towards the counsellor who is seen as obstructive and unhelpful – at best. In psychodynamic terms, splitting may come to the fore and this means that people are either good or bad, there is no half-way house. The following example illustrates the importance of protecting the student's privacy in the face of one parent's difficulties in accepting the necessarily confidential nature of counselling.

When Kerry made an initial appointment to see a counsellor she refused to give her surname. During her first session she said very little and answered questions with a minimum of detail. She was attentive, however, and frequently glanced over at the counsellor during the session, as though to keep her in sight. With little to go on the counsellor asked her if she would like to come back for another session. Kerry nodded in agreement and left without a further word. She was slightly more forthcoming at the next session though she still refused to give her surname or say why she wanted counselling. Over the course of a further two sessions, through her comments about Kerry's obvious anxiety about revealing anything about herself, the counsellor was able to make some emotional contact with her though she did not know what Kerry's subsequent tears were about. A few days later the counsellor had a telephone call from an irate parent demanding to know if his daughter was seeing a counsellor at the university. His description of his daughter, who had some unusual physical features, left no doubt that he was Kerry's father. The counsellor explained that the counselling service had a strict policy of confidentiality and that she was unable to answer his query. Kerry began her next session by reporting that her father had told her that he had spoken to a counsellor at the university who had said that she had seen Kerry. He told her that he had then demanded to know what they had talked about. The counsellor confirmed that her father had telephoned and repeated what she had told her father. After a few minutes of silence Kerry began to sob, her shoulders shook as she tried to contain her feelings and eventually she lost control and wept openly. In the following weeks Kerry gradually spoke more about herself and eventually told her counsellor about how she had been raped by a colleague of her father who had stayed with them while on a business trip last year. Her mother was a rather weak woman whom she had never felt close to; her father had a violent temper and she had been afraid of how he might react if he ever found out. On a recent visit home, she had confided in her mother that she had been feeling depressed and had seen a counsellor; her mother had told her father who had then demanded to know from Kerry why she was seeing a counsellor. When Kerry refused to answer him he had rung the counselling service. Over the following months, Kerry slowly worked out her feelings about what had happened to her and towards the end of her counselling she revealed how important it had been to her that the counsellor had not told her father about her counselling.

In this example, it is clear that the counsellor's protection of the student's privacy was central to the establishment of a relationship between them within which the student felt sufficiently secure to begin to explore her feelings. While confidentiality is not often as visible an issue as in this case, it is nonetheless vital and its preservation an essential element of the process of counselling.

The student counsellor

While the aim of this book has not been to 'teach' student counselling, but rather to introduce a particular psychological model for thinking about the problems that students encounter during their time at university, some readers may be interested to know more about the background and training involved in becoming a student counsellor. This short section is addressed to this issue.

At the time of writing, there is no statutory requirement for counsellors or psychotherapists to be registered in order to practise. There are, however, a number of regulatory bodies with which counsellors and psychotherapists can voluntarily register and most student counsellors belong to one of these. In addition, many student counsellors are members of the Association for University and College Counsellors, a sub-division of the British Association for Counselling.

As with most specialist areas within counselling and therapy, there is no formally recognised post-qualification training in student counselling in the United Kingdom and student counsellors are an extremely heterogeneous group with regard to their professional qualifications and backgrounds. In addition to their formal training in counselling or psychotherapy, some student counsellors have professional qualifications in the 'helping professions' such as medicine, clinical psychology, social work, nursing and so forth, while others have previously worked as teachers or administrators in further or higher education. Many student counselling services require their counsellors to have at least a qualification in counselling or psychotherapy that is recognised by the British Association for Counselling, the United Kingdom Council for Psychotherapy or the British Confederation of Psychotherapists. Generally speaking, psychotherapy trainings tend to be both more intensive and extensive in their requirements of their students than counselling trainings. Previous relevant experience is also usually considered as a basic requirement by most counselling services; for example, therapeutic work with young people. A number of student counselling services offer supervised placements to counsellors in training and this is one means by which direct experience in this area can be gained.

As will have become apparent from many of the examples described throughout this book, student counsellors often have to deal with students with very serious psychological problems and, not uncommonly, they are the first port of call for such students. 'Working at the coal face', as many student counsellors do, requires particular qualities which are, in the main, slowly developed through a combination of lengthy training and practice. While a capacity to empathise with students and their situation is important, having been a university student oneself is *not* sufficient in itself to equip one for working in this field. Most reputable counselling and psychotherapy trainings require their students to undergo personal therapy; this experience, alongside their theoretical training and clinical practice, provides the counsellor with the solid foundation that enables them to understand and withstand the emotional strain and rigours of dealing on a daily basis with individuals who often present in deeply distressed states. Finally, it is worth remembering that many students are just beginning their lives as young and independent adults and the job of helping them negotiate the emotional difficulties they encounter *en route* can be immensely rewarding.

Further reading

Bell, E. (1996) *Counselling in Further and Higher Education*, Buckingham: Open University Press.

Lees, J. and Vaspe, A. (eds) (1999) *Clinical Counselling in Further and Higher Education*, London: Routledge.

Tonnesmann, M. (1980) Adolescent re-enactment, trauma and reconstruction, *J. Child Psychother.* vol.6.

Whitaker, D. S. (1985) *Using Groups to Help People*, London: Routledge and Kegan Paul.

POSTSCRIPT

In this book I have endeavoured to provide a model of psychological development within which to explore some of the more common problems experienced by students at university. However, limitations of space have, inevitably, led to the relative neglect of some other significant areas, for example, the particular concerns of mature students, overseas students and disabled students. To address these in an adequate fashion would require a proper consideration of the particular context from within which these students enter higher education and is beyond the scope of this book. In the case of mature students, for instance, the relevant developmental issues in understanding the problems that affect them as students extend well beyond adolescence; for example, some mature students experience difficulties in adjusting from the position of employee to that of student, especially if their previous job involved significant responsibilities. Feelings stirred up by the loss of their former identity and authority, along with feelings of inadequacy in relation to much younger students who have not had a break from full-time education, can also become problematic. Many mature students have family commitments and these also impact on their potential experience as students; and so on. As with mature students, the experiences of overseas students and disabled students are informed by their particular circumstances and the difficulties they might encounter at university cannot be properly comprehended without examining the psychological implications of their situation; in the case of overseas students this would obviously include an appreciation and understanding of the emotional sequelae of leaving one's homeland and settling in a foreign country.

Another issue which I have only touched upon briefly is that of the growing impact of financial considerations upon the lives of students. The introduction of mandatory contributions towards fees and the gradual erosion of student grants have meant that many more students have had to take up part-time paid employment to support themselves while at university. This issue cannot be separated from the move towards widening access in higher education advocated by the government. While laudable in its general aims, the lack of a commensurate increase in resources to universities to meet increased student numbers has led to a diminution in the educational and welfare support available for each student and recent reports from university counselling services suggest an increase in the level of psychological disturbance among university students.

Thus, while more people can now look forward to entering university and taking part in higher education, we have also to bear in mind the increasing stresses and strains that being a student nowadays may bring. In this book I have begun to explore some of the factors that contribute to the problems that students commonly experience; as I have intimated above, there are many more yet to be explored.

BIBLIOGRAPHY

Anderson, R. and Dartington, A. (eds) (1998) *Facing It Out: Clinical Perspectives on Adolescent Disturbance*, London: Duckworth.

Bateman, A. and Holmes, J. (1995) *Introduction to Psychoanalysis: Contemporary Theory and Practice* , London and New York: Routledge.

Bell, E. (1996) *Counselling in Further and Higher Education*, Buckingham: Open University Press.

Blos, P. (1962) *Adolescence*, New York: Macmillan.

Bowlby, J. (1969) *Attachment and Loss, vol. 1, Attachment*, London: Hogarth.

Bowlby, J. (1973) *Attachment and Loss, vol. 2, Separation*, London: Hogarth.

Bowlby, J. (1980) *Attachment and Loss, vol. 3, Loss*, London: Hogarth.

Brown, D. and Pedder, J. (1993) *Introduction to Psychotherapy: An Outline of Psychodynamic Principles and Practice*, 2nd edn, London: Routledge.

Erikson, E. (1968) *Identity: Youth and Crisis*. New York: Norton.

Freud, A. (1936) *The Ego and the Mechanisms of Defence*, London: Hogarth.

Gorrell Barnes, G. (1998) *Family Therapy in Changing Times*, London: Macmillan.

Hinshelwood, R. D. (1994a) *Clinical Klein*, London: Free Association Books.

Laing, R. D. and Esterson, A. (1964) *Sanity, Madness and the Family*, London: Tavistock Publications.

Laufer, M. (Ed.) (1995) *The Suicidal Adolescent*, London: Karnac Books.

Laufer, M. and Laufer, E. (1984) *Adolescence and Developmental Breakdown*, New Haven: Yale University Press.

Lees, J. and Vaspe, A. (eds) (1999) *Clinical Counselling in Further and Higher Education*, London: Routledge.

Malan, D. (1979) *Individual Psychotherapy and the Science of Psychodynamics*, London: Butterworth.

Pincus, L. and Dare, C. (1978) *Secrets in the Family*, London: Faber and Faber.

Rayner, E. (1971) *Human Development*, Allen and Unwin, 3rd edn, 1986.

Rutter, M. (1972) *Maternal Deprivation Reassessed*, Harmondsworth: Penguin.

Sandler, J., Dare, C. and Holder, A. (1992) *The Patient and the Analyst*, 2nd edn, London: Karnac.

Sayers, J. (1998) *Boy Crazy: Remembering Adolescence, Therapies and Dreams*, London: Routledge.

Segal, H. (1973) *Introduction to the Work of Melanie Klein*, London: Hogarth.

Skynner, R. and Cleese, J. (1983) *Families and How to Survive Them*, London: Methuen.

Socarides, W. and Kramer, S. (eds) (1996) *Work and Its Inhibitions: Psychoanalytic Essays*, Madison: International Universities Press.

Stern, D. (1985) *The Interpersonal World of the Infant*, New York: Basic Books.

Tonnesmann, M. (1980) 'Adolescent re-enactment, trauma and reconstruction', *J. Child Psychother.*, vol.6.

Van Heeswyk, P. (1997) *Analysing Adolescence*, London: Sheldon.

Waddell, M. (1998) *Inside Lives: Psychoanalysis and the Growth of the Personality*, London: Duckworth.

Whitaker, D. S. (1985) *Using Groups to Help People*, London: Routledge and Kegan Paul.

Winnicott, D. W. (1971) *Playing and Reality*, New York: Basic Books.

Winnicott, D. W. (1972) *The Maturational Process and the Facilitating Environment*, London: Hogarth Press.

INDEX